Ancient India

A Captivating Guide to Ancient Indian History, Starting from the Beginning of the Indus Valley Civilization Through the Invasion of Alexander the Great to the Mauryan Empire

Free Bonus from Captivating History
(Available for a Limited time)

Hi History Lovers!

Now you have a chance to join our exclusive history list so you can get your first history ebook for free as well as discounts and a potential to get more history books for free! Simply visit the link below to join.

Captivatinghistory.com/ebook

Also, make sure to follow us on Facebook, Twitter and Youtube by searching for Captivating History.

Contents

Introduction

Ancient India was home to one of the oldest civilizations in the world: the Indus Valley civilization. But how did the Indian culture come to be?

Dive into the world of one of the first civilizations, and follow the rise of ancient India from Harappa and the first wave of urbanization to the first monarchial dynasty of Kuru. Discover how Buddha went from being a wealthy prince to one of the greatest and most appreciated religious figures in the history of spiritualism. Find out why Alexander the Great fell in love with India and how he was prevented from becoming the king of the world. You will learn why Ashoka the Great was the greatest king in the history of India and how his grandfather Chandragupta formed the biggest empire in the world.

And amidst the battles for dominion over the Indo-Gangetic Plain and the Indus River, you will read about how the common people of ancient India lived. What did a day in the life of an average Mauryan look like? What did people of ancient India eat, how did they dress, and what did they believe?

Find all these answers and more in *Ancient India: A Captivating Guide to Ancient Indian History, Starting from the Beginning of the Indus Valley Civilization Through the Invasion of Alexander the Great to the Mauryan Empire!*

Chapter 1 – The Birth of a Great Civilization in the Fertile Indus Valley

A powerful and advanced civilization rose from the banks of the Indus River, by which India was named. The Indus Valley civilization emerged alongside some of the greatest ancient civilizations, such as Egypt and Mesopotamia.

Before excavations commenced, archaeologists believed that the Indus Valley civilization bloomed in the valley of the river Ganges and that it began with Aryan immigrants who came from central Asia and Persia around 1250 BCE. After finding new evidence with more excavations, historians and scholars could move the timeline to between 1800 and 1500 BCE, providing new context for the Indus Valley and the significance of the Indus River for the general development and evolution of the civilization that would become known as Harappan.

In the 19th century, India and the surrounding countries in the Indus Valley were all colonized by the British Empire. In 1856, British officials oversaw the construction of a railway, which was supposed to connect Karachi and Lahore, two cities located within the borders of modern-day Pakistan. As the construction went on, laborers kept finding old bricks that were baked in fires many years ago. The bricks were lodged as if someone had purposefully placed them there, and while the laborers used some of these bricks in the construction of the railway, it was soon evident that they were using priceless pieces of ancient history.

At first, archaeologists thought that the bricks belonged to the Maurya civilization. The Maurya Empire dominated the Indus Valley from around 322 BCE to 185 BCE. However, these fire-baked bricks were discovered to be much older. They had discovered the ancient city of Harappa.

One year after Harappa was discovered in Punjab, Mohenjo-daro was discovered in the northern province of Sindh in modern-day Pakistan. Translated, Mohenjo-daro means "the mound of the dead," although this meaning is often reputed. Some scholars believe that by the time Mohenjo-daro had become one of the two biggest centers of power, which was between 2500 and 1700 BCE, Harappa had already met its decline. Some even think that Harappa just succeeded Mohenjo-daro, hinting that the two main centers weren't contemporary. However, much of the evidence shows that they coexisted.

Further research and excavations led scholars to discover the ancient site of Mehrgarh. Mehrgarh is located in modern-day Pakistan in the Kacchi Plain in Balochistan, and it was first discovered by archaeologists in 1974. These excavations were completed by French archaeologists Jean-François Jarrige and Catherine Jarrige. This husband-and-wife duo provided scholars with evidence of a civilized ancient world that dates back to 7000 BCE. This revelation changed the way the Indus Valley civilization was perceived in terms of its development and significance in the ancient world.

And so, the very beginning of the Indus Valley civilization was discovered, and scholars were now able to start piecing together the picture of this ancient civilization.

The Beginning of the Indus Valley Civilization

The earliest evidence of the Indus Valley civilization dates back to 7000 BCE. As mentioned above, it was found in the Neolithic settlement of Mehrgarh, located to the west of the Indus Valley. The evidence shows that Mehrgarh was once a small farming village that was formed around 7000 BCE and thrived until 5500 BCE.

Around 7000 BCE, the Indus Valley civilization didn't use irrigation. Later on, the Indus people took up irrigation; it is presumed that their irrigation system was copied from the one used in Mesopotamia, as the two civilizations began trading with each other. There is also evidence that the settlement of Mehrgarh cultivated domesticated cotton around 5000 BCE.

The early Indus people relied on several types of wheat and barley. It is actually believed that barley was originally brought from Mesopotamia. Besides barley and wheat, people ate black gram (a kind of bean), mung beans, and pigeon peas. They also depended on sheep and goats. But even though the people had domesticated goats and sheep, the population relied on hunting. A great number of gazelle bones testify to this.

In the first stage of the Neolithic period in Mehrgarh, there were no ceramic tools. Instead, the people relied on wooden and stone tools, which mostly included knives made of stone with wooden handles. Excavations also revealed a limited number of ground stone axes.

Human burials showed signs of civilization in the second stage of the Neolithic period, which commenced around 5000 BCE. People were buried with necklaces that were made of stone beads or shells, and they would often be accompanied by baskets that were likely packed with food for the deceased. The burial tradition included sacrificing a young goat or sheep that would be buried together with the human remains.

While the people of the Indus Valley mostly built houses with mud bricks, a new type of building appeared during the transition from the first to the second stage of the Neolithic period. Small buildings, which were most likely used as granaries, became a common structure in the Indus Valley, indicating that the area went through improvements in agriculture as well as in architecture. The appearance of granaries was closely related to the use of irrigation, and the fact that there was a growing number of granaries at the beginning of the second stage of the Neolithic period indicates that the inhabitants often had a surplus in grain. Around 5000 BCE, a tectonic movement formed large quantities of silt, which created more fertile farmland.

There were some changes in domesticating animals around this time. People started to keep a humped variety of bovines known as zebu, which soon became more important and more common than goats and sheep. Later into the second stage, Mehrgarh people domesticated rice and made a greater number of tools, often using seashells and semiprecious stones. The use of stones, such as lapis lazuli and turquoise, indicate the beginning of trade with other civilizations, possibly Mesopotamia and surrounding settlements along the coast and in Central Asia. Pottery also became widely used in the second stage, and burials became more elaborate. People were now buried in pits that would be walled with mud bricks. The human remains would often be placed in these funerary chambers with clay figurines of a female. This figurine was most likely a primitive deity, possibly something similar to a Mother Earth figure.

Archeologists have also found remnants of tall brick walls, which may indicate that the people of Mehrgarh started to build monumental structures. The first use of ivory and copper is also noted in this period, while the growing population surely indicates that the Indus Valley civilization was booming. Mehrgarh wasn't the only settlement in the Indus Valley that showed such progress and advancement, although it was among the first settlements in the valley.

The transformation of the Indus Valley civilization is astounding. It started as a small settlement in Mehrgarh around 7000 BCE, and over time, the agricultural village evolved into a major civilization with two major cities—Harappa and Mohenjo-daro—and over a hundred smaller villages and settlements. These settlements could have been a part of the centralized governance of this area, something that was most likely first established in Harappa.

Chapter 2 – The Three Periods of Harappan Civilization

Harappa was a village in modern-day Punjab, Pakistan, west of the Ravi River in the Indus Valley. The Ravi River has since changed course, and it is now located to the north of the site.

The Harappan civilization, another name for the Indus Valley civilization, is periodically divided into three periods: Early Harappan (3300 BCE–2600 BCE), Mature Harappan (2600 BCE–1900 BCE, and Late Harappan (1900 BCE–1300 BCE). These divisions were created by scholars to differentiate the cultural, religious, social, and political development of the Harappan civilization.

What makes the Early Harappa period interesting to scholars is the appearance of what may be the first form of the Indus script. Clay tablets have been found that date from between 3300 BCE and 3200 BCE. The tablets contain trident-shaped and plant-like formations, which remind scholars of the Indus script.

During the first stage of the Early Harappan period, the Harappan people lived as farmers in the mountains. They would later descend into the valleys and continue with their agricultural practices and domestication of animals. The surrounding villages developed simultaneously with Harappa, later merging due to urbanization. At the end of the Early Harappan period, Harappa started to build walls around the city. There was more elaborate architecture, as well as and well-established trading routes and connections. By this time, the people of Harappa had domesticated the water buffalo and cultivated crops like peas, dates, and sesame seeds. Rice and cotton were also in use and domesticated.

During the transition between the Early and Mature periods, Harappan villages turned into urbanized cities, and their material culture started to develop, as scholars have discovered elaborate pottery styles and details from this period. What signifies the transition between the Early period and the Mature one is the appearance of stamp seals with the Indus script, which began to take its final form in 2600 (scholars date the fully developed Indus script to between 2600 and 1900 BCE).

By the end of the Early Harappan and the beginning of the Mature period, the people of the Indus Valley had already learned how to control the floods and use them in their favor. Instead of being washed away, the people would enjoy a surplus in crops and grain. Aside from Harappa by the Ravi River, archaeologists have found over 1,050 urban cities in the area of the Ganges dating from the Mature Harappan period.

With the Mature Harappan period, urbanization and urban planning across the valley took place, indicating the Indus Valley civilization's development. Granaries became more sophisticated and larger, with a separate room for pounding grain and making flour. There was also a distinct difference between homes, as some of these houses were more luxurious than others, which indicates that social classes had begun to form. The use of the first ancient urban sanitation systems is also noted; the people of the Indus Valley used hydraulic engineering to ensure clean water and proper sanitation. These systems are the first examples of urbanized sanitation in the ancient world.

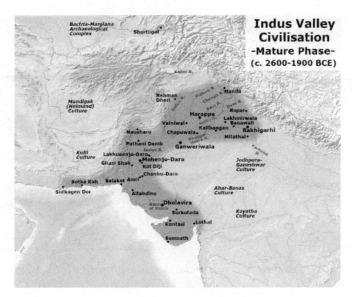

Mature Harappan period (2600-1900 BC). Credit: McIntosh, Jane (2008). The Ancient Indus Valley: New Perspectives.

Sophisticated drainage and reservoir systems ran across and underneath the city, with house drainages being connected to the city's main drainage system. Reservoir supplies were used for supplying the public and private baths. Judging by the elaborate water and drainage systems, the Indus Valley civilization placed a major emphasis on hygiene. The houses in the valley got drinking water from numerous wells dug around the wider location of Harappa and its surrounding urban centers. One well could have been used by a group of houses.

Even the smallest of houses had courtyards or smaller lanes leading to the entrance of the house. Aside from brick homes, the Indus people built tall brick walls that were most likely used to block incoming floods and neutralize the destructive effects that monsoons could inflict. The Mature Harappan period also saw new building structures, such as dockyards, warehouses, and brick platforms. One of the most exceptional buildings that have been found is the Great Bath, which was discovered in Mohenjo-daro.

The Great Bath in Mohenjo-daro, excavated in 1926. Credit: M. Imran, Wikimedia Commons.

The Great Bath is located on a mound that is known as the "citadel" and is estimated to have been built around the 3rd millennium BCE. It is known as the oldest example of a public water tank. The bath had two staircases, which led to two separate entrances into the bathhouse (one from the north, the other from the south). Along the eastern side of the bath, there is a series of rooms that stretch across the complex. Some of these rooms were probably used to supply the water tank, while one of them has a well.

It is unlikely that a building of such magnificence and space was used only as an everyday public bathhouse. Scholars believe that the Great Bath might have been used for religious purposes. After all, water is a symbol of purification in many cultures, and if that was the case here, this means that the purpose of the Great Bath was to purify and cleanse the bathers spiritually.

If one crossed the street from the Great Bath, one would find another massive building with two floors and several rooms. Scholars have compared the size of the Great Bath to the building across the street, as well as the proximity of the building. Many presume that this building used to house priests.

Although there was a priest class, most of the people living in the urban centers of the Indus Valley were either craftsmen, artisans, or traders. Highly valued tin-glazed beads and different ornamented vestiges have been found in excavations, testifying to trade networks across the wider area in the Indus Valley and outside in Central Asia.

When it comes to societal classifications, it seems that there was no distinct concentration of wealth in certain areas of the cities, as all the houses had the same access to wells and water supplies. However, the difference in the sizes of the houses proves that some people were wealthier than others.

Culture, Governance, Art, and Life in the Mature Harappan Period

Scholars can't find any evidence of an ultimate leader or powerful ruler or even the existence of a monarchy and hereditary power over a single political body in the Mature Harappan period. What is certain is that there was some sort of governance in place. It was most likely centralized or divided among the major urban centers, such as Mohenjo-daro and Harappa. People used standardized weights across the entire Indus Valley, and the cities in the valley resembled each other, which indicates that these cities might have been under centralized governance.

Scholars suggest that there were no distinctive social classes during the Mature Harappan period and that all citizens had equal rights and probably equal or nearly equal wealth. Similar vestiges found across the Indus Valley during this period, such as pottery, stamps, grid patterns for urbanization, brick sizes, building styles, symbols, statuettes, and the method of burial, all indicate that the over 1,050 cities of the valley were under a single government. The people of the Indus Valley most likely had their own rulers or government officials, but the area also might have been ruled by religious leaders as well. However, it is not known how these leaders might have been chosen or the extent of their power.

Since religion must have been an important part of the Indus Valley civilization, it is presumed that the region was ruled by priests who also had the role of gurus or teachers. They taught religion to young boys and girls from the age of five. Those same boys and girls enjoyed toys that were probably made by their parents; as stated above, most people in the urban centers were either artisans, craftsmen, or traders. The discovery of dice with dots that signify numbers indicates that adults also played games.

The surplus in grain and crops, thanks to the irrigation systems in place, provided the Indus Valley civilization with everything it needed to develop. That is how the people in this area were among the first in the ancient world to be able to accurately measure time, mass, and length. Besides being one of the first to come up with standardized weights, the Indus people used touchstones, small slate tablets, to test gold and its purity. They also introduced some novel techniques in metallurgy.

The people of the Indus Valley weren't only practical but also knew how to appreciate the aesthetic and beauty of everyday objects. They made pottery, ceramics, and stamp seals. They often depicted animals that could represent deities. A good example of an animal symbol that could have a religious meaning is found on an ancient seal dating from the Mature Harappan period, proving the existence of animistic polytheism. This seal depicts a zebu bull with massive horns on its head. What this animal is supposed to represent is still speculated among scholars; however, it is thought that the impressive seal with a zebu bull represents power and probably the most powerful clan in Harappa or Mohenjo-daro.

Ancient Indus seal depicting a zebu bull with large horns, probably originating from Harappa or Mohenjo-daro. Credit: The National Museum, New Delhi.

Another example of animal symbols is found on a seal depicting none other than a unicorn. It was one of the most common symbols used on seals in the Indus Valley. Although some people argue that unicorns might have existed and died out, it is much more likely that the usage of unicorns on these seals was in a mythical sense.

Unicorn seal, Mohenjo-daro. Credit: National Museum, Karachi.

Oftentimes, the unicorn has some bovine features and stands before an altar, which indicates that the seal might have been used for ritual purposes. The collar on the unicorn may indicate that the animal would have been used in sacrificial rituals. The seal might also represent a clan, similar to the zebu bull seal.

Aside from semiprecious metals, gold, and ceramics, the Indus people used terracotta, glazed steatite, agate, and shells to make jewelry, ornaments, and figurines that depicted humans, both male and female. They also made vessels out of terracotta, often painting animals such as monkeys, bears, cows, and dogs. These vessels were most likely used for ceremonial and religious purposes.

A great number of statuettes depicting female and male figures in motion have been found to match the Mature Harappan period. What differentiates these figurines from other types of artworks found in other urban centers at the time is the sophistication of movement and realistic postures and features. According to the director-general of the archaeological site in Mohenjo-daro, Sir John Marshall, "When I first saw them, I found it difficult to believe that they were prehistoric...I thought that some mistake must surely have been made; that these figures had found their way into levels some 3000 years older than those to which they properly belonged."

The Indus Valley civilization was indeed ahead of its time, not only in art but also in technology, architecture, and (most likely) comprehending the world and life through the lens of religion. Citadels and major buildings were being built and used for religious purposes, but there are no signs of buildings being used for the same purpose in Mesopotamia and Egypt during this period.

The Dancing Girl, bronze, Mohenjo-daro (2600-1900 BC). Credit: The National Museum of India, New Delhi, Wikimedia Commons.

As a testament of religion in the Indus Valley, there are over a thousand extracted stamp seals of various sizes and with different symbols depicted on them, many of which also have a form of the first Indus script. Some of these seals depict a human deity with animal features. A human deity with bull horns, a tail, and hooves might be a version of what is known as the "Lord of Animals," "Lady of Animals," or "Master" or "Mistress of Animals." The motif of a human mastering wild animals was common in this period, and it is noted in Egypt and Mesopotamia as well. One seal shows a human deity with bull features fighting a beast that looks like a tiger with horns. Humans mastering the wilderness, animals, and other natural elements were commonly depicted in art during this period.

Concerning the early forms of the Indus script, there is a question on what language the Indus people spoke. Scholars suggest that there might have been several languages in use, thanks to the Indus people's elaborate trading connections. However, it is believed that the Indus people spoke the proto-Dravidian language. Proto-Dravidian probably originated in Elam, and it was most likely brought to the Indus Valley by farmers who came from the Fertile Crescent.

As you can see, the Indus Valley civilization was advanced in regards to technology, art, and architecture. But the people of the valley were also advanced in transportation, as their economy mostly depended on trading. The Indus people might have been the first or among the first civilized nations to use wheels for transportation. They built ox carts to transport goods and people, and they also built small boats. At this time, the very beginning of relations between the Indus Valley and Mesopotamia was established. The Indus Valley also traded with Afghanistan, Persia, and likely Egypt and Crete.

History has shown that every civilization eventually meets its decline, which was the case in the Late Harappan period. Around 1900 BCE, a gradual decline commenced, and urban centers were being slowly abandoned by 1700 BCE. Archaeologists revealed that around this time, the people of the Indus Valley entered more conflicts on a local level, while infectious diseases like leprosy added to the overall deterioration of the Harappan people. More regional cultures emerged in the area, while the people of the Late Harappan period were experiencing hardship.

Although people still made art, the artwork seems diluted in comparison to the Mature Harappan period, with fewer sculptures and statuettes being found and with seals and art becoming less elaborate. Urban centers and urbanized areas were in decline with rural expansion across the Indus Valley, and trading also became less common. New buildings were still being erected; however, these buildings weren't as elaborate. The drainage and sanitation systems, as well as public baths, were no longer maintained, and it became evident that the Harappan civilization was about to end.

There is no clear answer as to what happened to the Indus people to cause this decline. There is a theory that Aryans invaded the region, but many scholars have dismissed it due to the lack of substantial, contextual, and material evidence. It is interesting to note that there is a complete lack of weapons in the Indus Valley, which contributes to the theory of the civilization's decline. It is unlikely that the Indus people could have avoided violent conflicts with other civilizations and cultures forever.

The answer might lay in the discovery of funerary pottery. Oftentimes, these were urns that depict a peacock with a human-like form inside of it, as well as the depiction of a hound. This hound might be the symbol of a deity that would be new to the region: Yama, the god of death in Hinduism and Buddhism. The emergence of this deity might signify the arrival of new cultural currents that led to a gradual decline of the Harappan people.

While there are theories of a new culture pushing out the Harappan people, it is unlikely to have been the direct cause of their decline. More than likely, the civilization's decline was due to several factors. The climate started to cool down significantly around 1800 BCE, which changed the way the rain and monsoons "fed" the land that nurtured the Harappans. With the climate shift, the river changed its course, and the general populace faced droughts. In combination with a decline in trading with Mesopotamia and Egypt, the people migrated toward the river Ganges, where they formed smaller urban settlements. The material culture also met its decline with the worsening living conditions, but the nation didn't completely disappear. Instead, the Harappan people thrived in other settlements in the Indus Valley from 1800 BCE to 325 BCE, which was when Alexander the Great invaded the Indian subcontinent.

The Last Stage of the Indus Valley Bronze Age

The culture known as the Ochre Colored Pottery culture thrived in the plains of the Ganges River, where the Harappan people ended up after the climate changes that struck the region around 1800 BCE.

The Ochre Colored Pottery culture represents the last stage of the Bronze Age in the Indus Valley civilization.

The Ochre culture thrived from around 2000 to 1500 BCE in the northern region of India in the area of Rajasthan. The originally unnamed and unknown culture that thrived in northern India was named after the ochre color that was left on the fingers of archaeologists who worked on excavations of pottery that had characteristic red and black details. Aside from ochre pottery, excavations unearthed copper vestiges and human-shaped statuettes and figurines similar to those found in Harappa and Mohenjo-daro. However, unlike in Harappa, archaeologists uncovered a hoard of weapons like double axes, flat axes, harpoons, and swords.

The Ochre culture is considered to have arrived with the Indo-Iranian wave of migration into the Indian subcontinent around the late 3rd millennium BCE. Based on the similarities in art, pottery, and the use of anthropomorphic statuettes, the Ochre culture shares some distinctive cultural characteristics with the coinciding development of the Harappan and post-Harapan period, the latter of which witnessed the emergence of Vedic culture.

In the last stage of the Bronze Age and the beginning of the Iron Age, Vedic culture emerged in the northern Indian subcontinent, forging new cultural achievements and ancient Indian literature that would survive the tooth of time.

Chapter 3 – The Iron Age in the Indus Valley: The Succession of Harappan

Sometime between 1300 and 900 BCE, one of the most significant pieces of Indian and Hindu culture was written: the Vedas. The period between 1500 and 500 BCE is known as the Vedic period since this was the time when Vedic literature was being composed. The Vedic period marked the timeframe of another booming culture, which was developing and living in the plains of the Ganges.

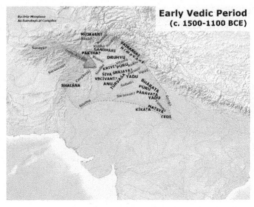

Early Vedic period (1500 to 1100 BCE). Credit: Wikimedia Commons.

The Vedas are religious and philosophical scriptures that represented the very core of knowledge for the ancient Indus people and are still relevant in Orthodox Hindu sects. They also stand as a testament to an important cultural and genetic connection between the Indo-Aryan people, who migrated to the Indian subcontinent, and Vedic culture. There isn't a group of people or a particular person who wrote and presented the Vedas to the Indus people.

The Vedic culture is characterized by the four parts of the Vedas, which were originally spread orally through precise narrations in the Old Indo-Aryan language long before the Vedas were ever written. It is not known when the Vedas were written; scholars presume that the Vedas were first recorded between 1500 and 500 BCE. Masters would teach their students about the Vedas, always emphasizing pronunciation so that all parts would be memorized and passed onto the next generation in the same form.

What is interesting about the Vedas is that its adherents believe they have existed forever. The Vedas explain the nature of the divine, while the word "Veda" itself means "knowledge." This body of texts is believed to have been sent from the world of the divine to sages, who received this sacred knowledge while in a state of long and deep meditation. The Vedas are among the oldest, if not the very oldest religious scriptures in the world.

The Vedas, Rig Veda, *written in Devanagari. Credit: Wikimedia Commons.*

Since the Vedas have been passed down through oral lore, these scriptures are also known as Shruti. When translated, Shruti means "what is heard." Another body of scriptures is known as Smriti, which means "what is remembered." The Smriti texts usually revolve around ancient heroes of Hindu culture and include literature such as *Bhagavad Gita, Ramayana,* and *Mahabharata.*

The Vedas consist of four scriptures: the *Rig Veda, Sama Veda, Yajur Veda,* and *Atharva Veda.* The scriptures are also divided into more detailed classifications based on the types of stories and texts written in the Vedas. These subdivisions are called Aranyakas, Brahmanas, Samhitas, and Upanishads. Aranyakas are texts with numerous observances on life and religion. Brahmanas are commentary texts related to rituals. Prayers, blessings, mantras, and benedictions are presented in the Samhitas, and Upanishads are narratives and dialogues that talk about the philosophy of the ancient Indus people, something that is still relevant in some Hindu sects.

It is believed that the very intonation of the words contained in the Vedas is the sound of the divine universe and that one could mimic the sounds of the universe by singing or reading the Vedas. That is why the translation of these sacred texts would annul a part of its meaning that was and still is considered divine in some Hindu sects.

Substantial parallels in the first Iranian religion, Zoroastrianism, which tracks its roots to ancient times, and the Vedas conclude that the Indo-Aryans and the Indus people of the Vedic culture are closely related, at least through spiritual beliefs. The theory makes even more sense when considering the Indo-Aryan migration into the Indian subcontinent. However, this theory is not accepted as a universal truth.

The Four Vedas and the Secret of Eternal Knowledge

The ancient people of the Indus Valley would ask questions about the meaning of life, their place in the world, and the nature of everything. How did the sun, celestial bodies, and all living beings come to be? How was everything created in its natural order? How can one become whole and be in unison with the divine? Reflective thoughts are the core of the Vedas.

The *Rig Veda* is comprised of ten mandalas, or books, that contain hymns to different gods, such as Agni (fire god) and Indra (storm god). These gods were eventually viewed as embodiments of Brahman, the source of all life. At the same time, Brahman is the end of everything—the very beginning and the very end of everything that exists. Wondering how, why, and what is strongly encouraged through the verses of the *Rig Veda.*

The *Sama Veda* represents the melody for the lyrics in the *Rig Veda*, as the texts in this Veda are almost completely taken from the *Rig Veda*. The *Sama Veda* is translated as "Song Knowledge" or "Melody Knowledge." The melody in the *Sama Veda* is supposed to be combined with a ceremonial dance, and together, it is believed to purify the soul and lift the spirit.

The *Yajur Veda*, the third Veda, is related to religious worship, and it contains chants and mantras. This Veda is also closely related to the *Rig Veda*, and it means "Ritual Knowledge" when translated.

When the name of the last Veda, the *Atharva Veda*, is translated, we get a glimpse into the legendary figure of the priest Atharvan. *Atharva Veda* means "knowledge of Atharvan," so most scholars believe that this Veda was written based on the magical and religious knowledge of Atharvan. The *Atharva Veda* contains magical spells, prayers, and rituals for everyday things. It also talks about how to ward off evil spirits and protect one's marriage. In addition, the Veda contains philosophical observations about life.

All four Vedas essentially explain life and its meaning through three divine figures: Brahma, Vishnu, and Shiva. Brahma is the creator of all existence and everything that lives, but he also represents life and existence itself. Vishnu is the preserver of life. Vishnu is supposed to protect the world and descend to Earth when the balance between good and evil is compromised. In the Hindu religion, it is believed that Vishnu was incarnated nine times since the universe's creation, and there is also the belief that this deity will descend among mortals once again before the world comes to an end. Shiva is the opposite of Vishnu, as the role of this deity is to destroy and bring havoc to the world. However, Shiva destroys the world only to recreate it. Shiva is not perceived as the ultimate opposite of Vishnu, as Shiva is both good and evil at the same time. Destruction is not always bad—sometimes, destruction is needed to create something better and more valuable, which means that destruction can also be beneficial and even necessary at times.

Brahma, Vishnu, and Shiva together make the holy triumvirate in the Hindu religion, and they are responsible for the world and life as it is—the good and the bad, destruction and creation. According to the Vedas, every person has a part of Brahma's, Vishnu's, and Shiva's essence within them, and their soul is contained within other deities as well, such as Agni, Indra, and Varuna. Agni represents the mouth and the voice of the gods and is the messenger between the divine and the mortal world on Earth. Agni means "fire," and this deity serves as the Hindu fire god. Indra is the god of thunderstorms and lightning. He is the ruler of the gods (Devas) and the king of heaven (Svarga). Varuna was originally the god of the skies, although he was later associated with water. Varuna is also the god of truth and justice and the father of Bhima and Hanuman. Bhima is mentioned in the *Mahabharata*, which is one of the most famous and well-known epics in the Vedas, and Hanuman is a deity that helps the god Rama and appears in the Vedas epic *Ramayana*.

The Vedas don't only tell a story about spirituality through insightful philosophical thought but also include important lessons and metaphors through epics such as the *Mahabharata* and *Ramayana*.

The *Mahabharata* tells a story about a battle for the throne and the Kurukshetra War, which involved two families, the Pandavas and Kauravas. This is the longest epic that was ever written, and all the events take place in the Indian subcontinent. This is where another major difference between the ancient Indus Valley civilization and the Vedic period can be found. During the dominance of the Indus Valley civilization by the Ravi River, there were no mentions of wars, conflicts, and battles, and archaeologists didn't find any weapons or signs of a battle in the region. On the other hand, the Vedas describe conflicts, battles for the throne, wars, and kings. The *Mahabharata* describes decades of war between the Pandavas and Kauravas, describing war strategies, weapons, and heroes in the battle for the throne of Hastinapur. However, despite the 100,000 lines dedicated to this war, scholars can't prove that any of the events are historically true.

Another war is mentioned in the *Rig Veda*, the Battle of the Ten Kings. This war will form a new tribe, the Kuru, which subsequently formed the Kuru Kingdom.

Wars, Battles, and the Kuru Kingdom

Before the Vedic period, there were no mentions of wars or kings, although the *Rig Veda* describes conflicts between the Aryans and the Dasyus and Dasas. Who were the Dasyus and Dasas? Dasas means "the servant of the gods," but it can also mean "enemy." Whether this name is a suffix or a representation of a metaphor is not yet clear to scholars. However, some scholars believe, including Asko Parpola, an Indologist and Sindhologist based in Finland, that the Dasyus and Dasas are the Dahyu and Dahae. These were Iranian tribes that penetrated northwestern India in the Early Vedic period and warred with the Aryans.

The *Rig Veda* tells about the various battles and bloody conflicts between the alienated tribes, one of which included the Bharatas, an Indo-Aryan tribe.

Bharata or Mahabharata (as mentioned in the applauded epic) is the legendary emperor of India. According to the epic in the *Rig Veda*, Bharata is the ancestor of Kurus, who later formed the Vedic Kuru Kingdom. As the epic describes, Bharata is both an ancestor of the Kauravas and Pandavas, the rival royal families in the *Mahabharata*. The legend of Bharata, who is unlikely to have existed in reality, states that he was born as the son of King Dushyanta and Shakuntala.

King Dushyanta loved to hunt and would often go on hunting trips. One day, he spotted a beautiful girl in the forest. This was Shakuntala, and he courted her, presenting her with a royal ring. Dushyanta had to go back to the capital of his kingdom, but he told Shakuntala to bring the ring with her to the royal court when she was ready to become his queen. Shakuntala gave birth to a healthy and strong baby boy who grew stronger each day. The baby was named Sarvadamana for his strength; the name means "the subduer of all." The *Mahabharata* continues to follow the life of Sarvadamana. Eventually, his name is changed to Bharata, which when translated means "cherished" or "the one who is cherished."

According to the epic, when Bharata was six years old, his mother decided to bring him before his father and claim her place as queen. The king was so embarrassed by Shakuntala's visit that he dismissed her claims and called her a liar. He refused to acknowledge her and their son. Divine forces interfered at this point, appearing in the royal court in the form of a voice that told King Dushyanta that he had to accept his son and Shakuntala. Bharata eventually succeeded his father and soon became the subduer of everything as far as the eye could see. He was strong and decisive, and he became a leader with unheard-of might.

Bharata married three wives who gave birth to nine sons; however, Bharata was disappointed, as none of his sons was fit to rule in his stead. His wives were so distraught that none of them could give birth to a worthy successor that they killed all their children. The sacrifice was so great that, when combined with Bharata's sacrifices by the Ganges River, it resulted in the birth of his adopted son, who would become the new king after his death. His name was Bhumanyu.

This legend intertwines historical facts that have been confirmed by historians and scholars, which takes us to tribal chief Sudas Paijavana, the leader of the Bharatas tribe during the Battle of the Ten Kings, which took place in the 2nd millennium BCE. The Battle of the Ten Kings is also described in the *Mahabharata* in detail. However, it remains unclear why the war started. It is presumed that the local chiefs fought for dominance over the rivers in the region, as rivers were important for irrigation.

Another theory states that the war between Sudas and the alliance of the ten tribal kings—Adu, Yadu, Puru, Tarvasa, Alina, Druhyu, Paktha, Bhalanas, Vishanin, and Siva—happened because Sudas decided to replace Vasishtha with another sage named Vishvamitra. Vasishtha is mentioned in the *Rig Veda* as being one of the oldest and most respected sages, while Vishvamitra is considered a semi-divine being.

According to a verse in the *Mahabharata*, Sudas decided to cross the rivers of Sutlej and Beas on his way to Kurukshetra, which was enough reason to start a battle with the alliance he encountered. Again, the exact reason for the war is not mentioned.

Scholars weren't able to retrieve the names of the tribes that Sudas fought in the Battle of the Ten Kings. However, some scholars believe that he could have battled some of the following tribes: the Purus, Yadu, Matsyas, Yaksu, Pakthas, Druhyus, Alinas, Bhalanas, Vishanins, Anu, Vaikarna, and Sivas.

Sudas won the battle, which resulted in his tribe merging with the Puru tribe. This merger, which created the Kuru, was the very beginning of the first state in India. The Kuru extended from modern-day Delhi to Punjab and Haryana; some parts of the state were also located in the area of western Uttar Pradesh. The Kuru tribal union eventually came to be known as the Kuru Kingdom.

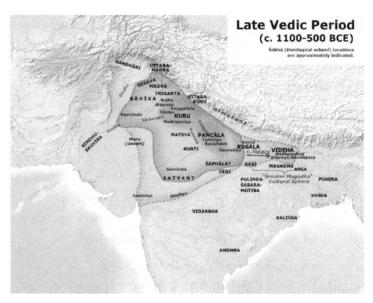

The Kuru Kingdom and surrounding kingdoms, Late Vedic period (1100 to 500 BCE). Credit: Wikimedia Commons.

The Kuru Kingdom was formed between 1200 and 800 BCE, and it is the first recorded center of power in the Indian subcontinent, with Hastinapur as its capital (at least for the majority of the kingdom's existence). The kingdom had a central authority based in the capital, but it was divided into regions and districts. Kuru Proper was a region in the Kuru Kingdom that was inhabited by the majority of the kingdom's subjects, and it was further divided into provinces, regions, and territories. Kurujangala was another region in the kingdom, and it was mostly covered in thick jungle. It was the home to the Jangala tribe, whose survival greatly depended on the flow of the Yamuna. Kurujangala was further split into three regions, one of which had three cities: Panaprashta, Swarnprastha, and Indraprastha.

Kurukshetra was the third area of the kingdom, and it had been the very place where Sudas came before the Battle of the Ten Kings. Kurukshetra was blessed with five rivers—the Oghavati, Saraswati, Hiranwati, Apaga, and Drisadhwati—and covered in vast plains.

The Kuru Kingdom's first capital was Indraprastha, at least according to literature sources after the Middle Vedic period. However, scholars claim that the first capital was Asandivat in Haryana.

The kingdom was mostly comprised of nomadic tribes and tribes that relied on domesticated animals. These tribes descended from the mountains before the Battle of the Ten Kings, shifting toward the plains of the Ganges. Pastoral and nomadic tribes shifted to agriculture, cultivating barley and rice. The tribes also started using iron, mentioned in literature as the "black metal."

Before the Middle Vedic period, during the Rigvedic times, the class system only recognized two classes: Arya and Dasa. Arya was the ruling class of conquerors who subdued the Dravidian people. Dravidians, who had origins from South Asia, were considered to be godless savages and were subjugated as the slave class in the Kuru Kingdom. Their language and dark complexion differentiated them from Aryans (not to be confused with the later definition of Aryan that Adolf Hitler supported—the Indo-Aryans came from a region called Aryavarta). There were also noted cultural differences.

In the Middle Vedic period, the class system became more elaborate, with the society of the Kuru Kingdom being divided into four classes: Brahmin, Kshatriya, Vaishya, and Shudra. Brahmin was the class of priests who were considered to be gurus, physicians, and intellectuals, as well as the guardians of sacred knowledge. Kshatriya represented the military aristocracy, as Kshatriyas were a class of warriors in the Middle Vedic period. They were second in the caste hierarchy after the Brahmins. Vaishya is the third class in the caste system of the Kuru Kingdom. Vaishyas were most commonly cattle keepers and farmers; however, this caste expanded to other careers over time, such as money lenders, traders, and even landowners. The fourth class in the Kuru Kingdom was the Shudras. According to religious texts used during this period, the purpose of this class was to serve the first three castes. Shudras were usually laborers and craftsmen.

It is said the four castes originated from a primeval man who is said to have created Brahmin from his mouth, Kshatriya from his arms, and Vaishya from his legs. The Shudras are said to have come from his feet, which also describe their caste role as servants to the other three social classes.

The Kings of the Kuru Kingdom

Of course, a kingdom couldn't be called a kingdom if there wasn't a king to rule it, so naturally, the Kuru Kingdom had a king, which was called a raja. The kingdom was rarely inherited by blood lineage; instead, the kings of Kuru were chosen by the Samiti, a tribal assembly in the early Rigveda period. The assembly also consisted of women. The importance of the Samiti deteriorated in the Late Vedic period, as there is evidence that the kingship became hereditary.

The king wouldn't have ruled the entire kingdom by himself, so scholars believe there was some kind of king's court in the Late Vedic period. The king would have ruled with a priest as his guide and advisor, while the royal court would have consisted of chieftains, an army chief, emissary, spies, heralds, and food distributors who helped the ruler with administration. The king would also organize frequent sacrifices to showcase his power and maintain the natural order in the caste system, with which they had help from Brahmin priests.

The king would also choose several tribunes among the common people as well as from subdued tribes. These tribunes would be sent to nearby tribes and kingdoms to pillage and raid, which was a great way to increase wealth and assert dominance in neighboring territories. One of the most common ways of asserting dominance in northern India was by the Ashvamedha. The Ashvamedha is a horse sacrifice specifically performed by newly elected kings. The king would send a horse around the kingdom for a year, and it would be accompanied by several warriors. Anyone in the kingdom could challenge the warriors for a year, and if no warrior was defeated, the horse would be returned to the king in the capital, where he would sacrifice the horse and confirm his authority and dominance.

The *Mahabharata* is used as the main source for studying the royal succession throughout the Vedic era of the Kuru Kingdom. The characters in the *Mahabharata* can't be historically confirmed with certainty, so this makes the epic a unique source of legends and myths that potentially intertwine with reality.

One of the most prominent Kuru kings mentioned in the *Mahabharata* is Parikshit, who ruled in the Middle Vedic period between 1100 and 800 BCE. Parikshit and his son, who inherited his father's throne, are said to be responsible for strengthening the dominance of the kingdom. Parikshit is further described in the Vedas as the king who made the darkness go away and brought prosperity and abundance to the kingdom. He had a long reign of twenty-four years and lived to be sixty; however, scholars cannot confirm this as a reliable historical fact. Parikshit is also known as the "universal king" in the *Mahabharata*, as everyone lived happily and in abundance during his reign.

It remains unknown how Parikshit died. His death revolves around a myth described in the Vedas. Parikshit went hunting. He was tired and unable to track the deer he had been hunting the entire day. So, he stopped to ask a sage named Shamika if he had seen the deer. Shamika was in a deep state of meditation, so he didn't give Parikshit an answer to his question. Parikshit was impatient and angry with Shamika, so he took a dead snake and placed it around Shamika's neck.

Shamika had a son named Sringin, and he was furious about what had happened. Sringin cursed Parikshit to die in seven days from a snakebite. Parikshit made peace with his death, but an effort was still made to protect the king by having all the king's ministers build a massive mansion that would stand on a single pole so that no snake could approach it. Parikshit retreated to the mansion and was well guarded, but it was all in vain as the king of all snakes, Takshaka, arrived.

The death of Parikshit, a scene from the Birla Razmnama *where Takshaka is shown biting Parikshit. Author unknown. Credit: Wikimedia Commons.*

Since Parikshit was guarded in a mansion that rested on a single pole, Takshaka couldn't get to him, especially since he also had to get past the king's guards. Takshaka turned into an insect and hid in the fruit that was served to Parikshit. When the king lifted the fruit to his mouth, the snake bit him.

To save the king, his ministers called upon a sage who could cure snake bites, Kashyapa. Takshaka offered Kashyapa more wealth if he chose not to save the king, which the sage accepted. The Pandavas led a battle against Takshaka, while Parikshit's son, Janamejaya, promised to slay Takshaka within seven days from his father's death. He wanted to sacrifice the snake king; however, the divine Indra stopped Janamejaya in his attempt. This day is remembered as the celebration of Nagas—snakes—known as Naga Panchami.

Janamejaya is described in the *Mahabharata* as a conqueror and a great king, with numerous conquests and raids to the south and east. Janamejaya abdicated despite the potency he had as a king and warrior. The reason behind his abdication was a dispute he had with Vaisampayana, the narrator of the *Mahabharata,* one of the authors of the Vedic texts, and an ancient Indian sage. According to some sources, Janamejaya's throne was succeeded by his son, Satanika, while other sources note that the new successor was Janamejaya's grandson, Asvmedhadatta.

During Janamejaya's reign, the Kuru Kingdom became the main political and cultural power center in the northern part of the Indian subcontinent. The lineage of the Kuru kings, which consisted of both Kauravas and Pandavas, continued with the consolidation of the kingdom until the fateful shift of power around 500 BCE when the kingdom fell. After the rule of Parikshit, twenty-seven kings ruled the Kuru Kingdom, with Kshemaka being the last king.

The history of the Kuru Kingdom and its prominent kings remains veiled in myths and legends. The *Mahabharata* remains the richest source of knowledge about the Kuru dynasty, even though a great part of the Vedic stories can't be confirmed as historical facts.

The scene shows the sacrifice of Sarpa Satra (a sacrifice that would destroy all snakes), with Astika (a sage) stopping Janamejaya from destroying Takshaka and the other Nagas. Author unknown. Credit: Wikimedia Commons.

Chapter 4 – The Demise of the Kuru Kingdom and the Shift of Power in Ancient India

The Kuru Kingdom was founded in the aftermath of the Battle of the Ten Kings around 1200 BCE and found its demise around 500 BCE.

The Kuru Kingdom wasn't an isolated center of power, as neighboring states in the region of the Ganges bloomed into prominent kingdoms. With the demise of the Kuru Kingdom, the power shifted to other parts of the Indo-Gangetic Plain during the Late Vedic period. The kingdom of Panchala was one of the strongest kingdoms in ancient India, lasting from between 900 BCE and 500 BCE. Panchala was located in Doab, which is a land region between the Ganges and the Yamuna. Panchala had strong diplomatic relations with the Kuru Kingdom and emerged as a power center east of Kuru. According to scholars, Panchala was formed out of multiple tribes, including the Krivi tribe that might have come to this region from the Indus River plain.

By the end of 500 BCE, Panchala ceased to exist as a kingdom and transformed into an oligarchy as a part of the Solasa Mahajanapadas. The Mahajanapadas were an oligarchic coalition, while "Solasa" means sixteen. Kuru wasn't a part of the Mahajanapadas, as the kingdom had already found its demise with the arrival of the Salvi tribe, also known as Salva.

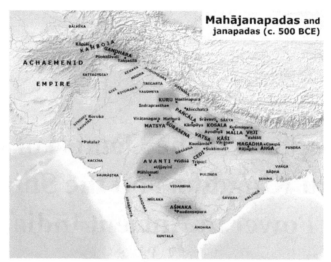

The Mahajanapadas in the post-Vedic period around 500 BCE.
Credit: Wikimedia Commons.

Scholars can't confirm with certainty from where the Salva came. However, they can link the origin of the Salva to the Trigarta Kingdom, located in the northern area of India and ruled by the Katoch dynasty. Trigarta is also mentioned in the *Mahabharata*, together with Panchala and the remaining states in the Mahajanapadas at the end of the Vedic period.

After the invasion of the Kuru Kingdom, the Salva tribe took over the area around the Yamuna River, where it soon became a dominant force. The Salva settled near the Matsya Kingdom, which was one of the sixteen Mahajanapadas. Kuru wasn't entirely decimated, as its people survived and later combined with the Salva and the Kingdom of Surasena, another one of the Mahajanapadas.

A coin found in Surasena, dating between 400 BCE and 300 BCE.
Credit: The British Museum, Wikimedia Commons.

Although the Salva was a non-Vedic tribe, they accepted Sanskrit and merged with the local culture in ancient India. Eventually, they assimilated with the local Vedic Mahajapanada of Surasena and what was left of Kuru. In the post-Vedic period, as the *Mahabharata* testifies, the Salva tribe accepted the teachings of the Vedic gurus.

However, despite the case of assimilation of the invasive Salva with one of the Mahajanapadas, the sixteen kingdoms remained quite diverse. The Mahajanapadas essentially represented small tribal kingdoms, which all emerged in the Late Vedic and post-Vedic periods.

In this melting pot of political and cultural differences, the tribal kingdoms gathered around the same religion and spiritual principles. Aside from the sixteen kingdoms, which were the most powerful in the Indo-Gangetic Plain, numerous tribal republics bloomed in the region. These prominent forces would soon be replaced with a new political and cultural power: the Mauryan Empire.

The Sixteen Mahajanapadas

Mahajanapadas, also known in the written form as the Maha Janapadas, is translated as the "great country" in Sanskrit, which partly explains their political and cultural significance in ancient India.

In the beginning, the Mahajanapadas were perhaps an accidental coalition between various tribal states and kingdoms that emerged in the plains of the Ganges and Indus. Over time, though, they became a significant political body with multiple independent authorities. The Mahajanapadas were formed around 600 BCE, coinciding with the deterioration of the Kuru Kingdom, which was taken over by the Salva tribe. The kingdoms that formed the Mahajanapadas were not any less invasive in comparison to the Salva, as these kingdoms expanded politically and territorially by taking land and raiding.

The sixteen kingdoms of Mahajanapadas were Anga, Assaka, Avanti, Chedi, Gandhara, Kamboja, Kashi, Kosala, Kuru, Matsya, Magadha, Malla, Panchala, Surasena, Vamsa, and Vajji.

Anga was one of the main cities in ancient India, and it was located in the present-day region of western Bengal and Bihar. Anga became one of the sixteen oligarchic republics in the second wave of urbanization that shifted from the Indus to the Ganges. Anga was an important trading center in ancient India, as was Assaka, which was located in present-day Maharashtra in central India.

One of the kingdoms that later became a part of the Mauryan Empire was Avanti. It was one of the spiritual centers of Buddhism and was divided into two provinces that had a natural border in the form of the river Vetravati (Betwa). The Chedi clan was one of the oldest in ancient India. It is mentioned in the old scriptures of the *Rig Veda* and was divided into two different settlements. One of the settlements was located near the Yamuna River, and the other bloomed in the mountains of Nepal.

The Gandhara had existed as a tribe since the beginning of the Vedic period. The Gandhara were known for being rather aggressive; they were very familiar with warfare.

The Kamboja tribe, which later became one of the sixteen Mahajanapadas, was mentioned as early as the Gandhara, as they were set on both sides of the Hindu Kush. Kamboja was an Indo-Iranian tribe that came to the region in the first wave of urbanization.

The Kashi settled around Varanasi, which got its name from the two rivers surrounding it, the Varuna and Assi. Kashi was the most powerful kingdom of all the Mahajanapadas until the emergence of Buddhism.

Kosala was located near the river Ganges from the south and surrounded by the Himalayas in the north, while another river, the Gandaki, marked the natural border of the kingdom in the east. Kashi merged with Kosala after the rise of Buddhism in the 5th century BCE and was later part of the Mauryan Empire. In the 5th century BCE, Kuru transformed into a republic and became one of the Mahajanapadas after the Salva invasion.

Matsya once belonged to the kingdom of Chedi. Matsya eventually gained its autonomy and became one of the sixteen prominent kingdoms in ancient India, taking the territory of Jaipur, Bharatpur, and Alwar.

Magadha emerged as a strong but loathed kingdom in present-day Bihar. This was due to the fact that Magadhas weren't Brahmins. Despite its ill-disposed status among other Brahmin kingdoms, Magadha was still one of the strongest kingdoms in ancient India.

Malla is often mentioned in the Buddhist scriptures, as Buddha spent his last day in one of the nine provinces of Malla, where he had his last meal as well. Malla is also described as one of the strongest tribes in India.

The Panchalas settled east from the Kuru tribe between the river Ganges and the Himalayas. Panchala was initially a monarchy and relied on the rule of a king; however, it later transformed into a republic in the 5th century BCE with the coalition of the sixteen oligarchic republics.

Surasena was one of the chief kingdoms during the rise of Buddhism. One of the kings of Surasena, Avantiputra, was also one of Buddha's main disciples, and he promoted the sacred knowledge of Buddhism throughout the kingdom.

In the deep north of ancient India was Vajji or Vriji, which was one of the most influential kingdoms among the Mahajanapadas around the 5th century BCE. Vajji consisted of nine different tribes, and it was an important center of Buddhism. It helped spread Buddha's doctrine and spiritual philosophy.

Vamsa, also known as Vatsa, is an offspring republic derived from the Kurus. It occupied the territory around present-day Allahabad in Uttar Pradesh. Its richest and most powerful city was the capital of Kaushambi. Kaushambi was one of the main power centers in the region, with numerous merchants residing there. The capital grew to be prosperous thanks to the fact that it was a natural strategic center of imported and exported goods, as well as a favorite stop of travelers coming from the south and northwest. Udayana was the king of Vamsa during the time of Buddha. He was a powerful ruler and one of Buddha's followers. Udayana promoted Buddhism and made it the main religion of his kingdom.

The Teachings of Siddhartha Gautama and Buddhism in Ancient India

Alongside the coalition of the sixteen oligarchic republics, a novel spiritual philosophy was born independently through the teachings of Siddhartha Gautama, who later became known as Buddha, meaning "awakened one" or "enlightened one." Siddhartha was born to an old noble family called the Shakya. The Shakya inhabited the area of Greater Magadha during the Vedic period, and their origins can be traced back to the 1ˢᵗ millennium BCE.

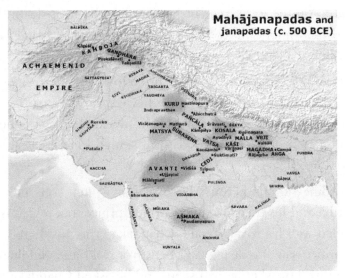

Ancient India during the time of Buddha, around 500 BCE. Credit: Wikimedia Commons.

The Shakya formed an oligarchic republic with the capital in Kapilavastu, where Siddhartha was raised. Siddhartha was born to a Shakyan oligarch named Suddhodana and his wife, Queen Maya. The Shakyas mostly depended on the rice they cultivated, so it is no wonder that the name of Suddhodana is translated as "the one who grows pure rice."

Suddhodana is often mentioned as a king in later scriptures, but it is unlikely that Buddha's father was an autocratic leader, i.e., a monarch. Shakya was probably run by a small elite group that had the power to vote for a leader, known as the raja. Suddhodana might have been a raja, as the references to Buddha's father mention him being the Shakyan king. Siddhartha himself also carried the title of prince before becoming the Enlightened One.

Siddhartha was born in Lumbini, located in modern-day Nepal in Lumbini Province. Lumbini translates to "the lovely" and is one of the most important pilgrimages for Buddhists. Scholars and historians can't agree on the exact year of Siddhartha's birth or death, but it is assumed that Siddhartha Gautama lived between 563 BCE and 483 BCE or between 480 BCE and 400 BCE.

Siddhartha was brought up in luxury. However, after witnessing the four sights—an old man bent due to his age, an ill person, a corpse, and an ascetic wandering the world—he decided to leave the palace and lead a stern life in the woods with some of the greatest gurus of the time.

According to numerous biographies written on the life of Siddhartha and his transformation from a prince to a religious leader, he traveled with his royal servant, Chandaka, who was there when the young prince saw the aging man bent from old age. Siddhartha was deeply moved by what he had seen, and he asked Chandaka about it. Chandaka explained that a part of life was growing old.

After seeing the four sights, Siddhartha woke up in the middle of the night, troubled by what he had witnessed. He then saw his four servants asleep around him. Their postures appeared eerie and unnatural to Siddhartha, as they all looked dead. He decided to leave the palace in the middle of the night with Chandaka and his white horse, Kanthaka. He was twenty-nine when he decided to live as an ascetic, leaving his wife, Yasodhara, and his son, Rahula, behind. The sights he had seen all revolved around suffering, and they made Siddhartha leave his life of comfort and privilege in search of answers that would decipher the meaning of human life and justify the suffering he had witnessed.

However, before he joined the ascetic gurus, Siddhartha left Chandaka and his horse, cut off his hair, and crossed the river Anomiya (Anoma). During his time with the gurus, Siddhartha realized that he couldn't find the answers to his questions and that he couldn't be released from suffering by renouncing all bodily pleasures and practicing severe self-denial and restraint. Siddhartha also knew from experience that a life of extreme luxury wouldn't create a life free of suffering. Neither lifestyle provided the answers he was seeking, so Siddhartha decided that the key to spiritual freedom was a balance between the two.

Siddhartha Gautama's epiphany signified the beginning of a new chapter for himself and spirituality in ancient India. His departure from his home and the comfort of his palace was considered to be a great sacrifice; this act is known as the Great Renunciation.

Siddhartha also encountered King Bimbisara, who was the ruler of Magadha, one of the great Mahajanapadas, while he was in Rajgir collecting money, food, clothes, and other items for those in need. Siddhartha was still on his journey toward enlightenment when Bimbisara offered him a part of his kingdom. Although Siddhartha refused to take a part of Magadha, he promised Bimbisara that his kingdom would be the first place he would visit once he found enlightenment.

Aside from being a great protector and a friend of Buddha, Bimbisara also indirectly laid the foundations of the later Maurya Empire by expropriating the kingdom of Anga, which was also one of the sixteen Mahajanapadas.

The scene of Bimbisara offering Siddhartha a part of his kingdom.
Credit: Hintha, Wikimedia Commons.

Bimbisara was later imprisoned by his son and heir, Ajatashatru. Bimbisara killed himself while in prison in 493 BCE. According to tradition, it is thought that Bimbisara is burning in hell due to taking his own life. He waits there until he is finally reincarnated.

Ajatashatru was also a contemporary of Buddha. In fact, Magadha reached its peak during his reign. Ajatashatru conquered many of the neighboring kingdoms, including Kosala, Kashi, and a great number of smaller kingdoms in the region. Ajatashatru was very talented when it came to warfare, and he even invented new weapons, a scythed chariot, and an engine that would hurl massive stones onto his opponents' armies and city walls. He was the most powerful ruler in North India, reigning from 492 BCE to 460 BCE.

The depiction of Ajatashatru during a nighttime visit to Buddha in search of advice from the Enlightened One. Credit: Wikimedia Commons.

Ajatashatru also met Buddha, but unlike his father, he met the Enlightened One after he had found enlightenment. Ajatashatru felt guilty for slowly poisoning his father while he was imprisoned and for being the reason behind his demise, so he decided to pay a visit to Buddha and ask for forgiveness. He wanted to be relieved of his suffering. Buddha forgave Ajatashatru, replying to his confession of sin, "Indeed, King, a transgression overcame you when you deprived your father, that good and just king, of his life. But since you have acknowledged the transgression and confessed it as is right, we will accept it. For he who acknowledges his transgression as such and confesses it for betterment in future, will grow in the noble discipline."

Buddha continued with his sacred teachings in the plains of the river Ganges, teaching noblemen as well as commoners about enlightenment and freedom from suffering for more than twenty years. After two decades of living as an ascetic, Buddha is said to have settled in the Kingdom of Kosala, spending most of his later years in the city of Shravasti.

The number of sangha followers also grew with the influence of Buddha and his spiritual teachings. Sangha refers to an assembly of Buddha's followers, which included men, women, and children who lived by the spiritual lessons of Buddhism.

Already old and in need of more rest, Buddha began to spread spiritual wisdom to his chief disciples. One of the greatest challenges for Buddha at this point was the rupture between him and his cousin Devadatta, who wanted to take over the role of the spiritual leader. After gathering a group of monks, Devadatta left the sangha and founded a new spiritual sect that would rival the Buddhist sangha. Some sources note that Devadatta plotted and tried to kill Buddha but with no success. Scholars still cannot agree on why Buddha and his cousin disagreed.

The last year of Buddha's life coincides with one of Ajatashatru's war campaigns. Ajatashatru led the kingdom of Magadha against Vajji, which was one of the Mahajanapadas. The *Mahaparinibbana Sutta,* one of the Buddhist scriptures, describes Buddha's encounter with one of Ajatashatru's ministers who came to Buddha to ask for his advice regarding the war against the Vajji.

It is important to note that at the time, Buddha lived as a spiritual leader and an ascetic who didn't conform with regular social and political situations in ancient India. Another important note is that Buddha promoted nonviolence. Instead of giving direct advice, Buddha mentions the Seven Conditions of Welfare, the Sapta Aparihani Dhamma. The Seven Conditions of Welfare that should be incorporated into a Buddhist community are devotion, modesty, conscientiousness, learning, persistent energy, mindfulness, and wisdom.

By proposing this, Buddha didn't speak against or in favor of the war against the Vajji. He showed compassion for the people of the Vajji even though he didn't warn them directly about the danger. Buddha intended to buy time for the Vajji, suggesting to Ajatashatru's chief minister that they should give the Vajjis at least three years to adopt the Seven Conditions of Welfare.

Shortly after this event, Buddha, who was already old and withering, although his health was noted to improve in the last months of his life, was asked by Ananda to choose his religious successor. Ananda was one of the ten chief disciples of Buddha and is also known as the treasurer of dharma, Buddha's teachings, as he had the best memory of all his disciples. Ananda was often an intermediary between Buddha and the sangha. Buddha explained to his faithful disciple that the order should not have any successors as long as the monks live by dharma.

Although he was already eighty years old, Buddha recovered from his illness and set off to teach and travel with Ananda. On his journey, he met a blacksmith named Cunda, who offered Buddha a meal, which the Enlightened One gratefully accepted. Shortly after having the meal, which would be his last, Buddha got ill once again. Cunda was worried that the meal he offered to Buddha had caused the illness, but Buddha told Ananda that he must convince Cunda that his meal granted him the energy he needed to finish his journey.

Buddha continued to travel and teach even after he got ill until he could no longer move. They had to stop in Kushinagar, a town in Uttar Pradesh, where Ananda had prepared a resting place for his teacher. On his deathbed, Buddha told his disciples that once he was gone, their teachers would be the Dharma-Vinaya, Buddha's teachings. Buddha took his last breath, with his last words being, "All formations decay. Strive for the goal with diligence."

Chapter 5 – Between the Empires of Ancient India

The Mahajanapadas was the dominant coalition in India until 345 BCE.

One of the main factors that led to the disintegration of the Mahajanapadas was the expansion politics of the Magadha kingdom during Bimbisara's reign. Bimbisara's son, Ajatashatru, had an even more aggressive strategy of expanding the kingdom's territory by force. Ajatashatru conquered the kingdoms of Kosala and Vajji and became the most powerful king among the sixteen oligarchic republics.

Ajatashatru was succeeded by his son Udayabhadra, also known to history as Udayin. Udayin ruled between 460 BCE and 444 BCE. Udayin was responsible for his father's death, just as Ajatashatru was the cause of his father's death. However, Udayin wasn't killed by his successor, breaking the tradition of patricide in the Haryanka dynasty.

Udayin often battled with the king of the neighboring Avanti, Palaka, and defeated his opponent on numerous occasions. However, Udayin was ultimately killed by Palaka. He was succeeded by Anurudha, whose relationship with Udayin is not clear to historians. It is certain that Udayin had no children. Anurudha probably ruled for only four years, from 444 BCE to 440 BCE, after which he was succeeded by Munda, who ruled from 440 BCE to 437 BCE.

Munda had a son named Nagadasaka, who would become the last ruler of the Haryanka dynasty. He ruled from 437 BCE to 413 BCE. He was deposed, and his minister, Shishunaga, took his place.

The Shishunaga dynasty was named after its founder, Shishunaga. He ruled the largest and most powerful kingdom in North India. Shishunaga was remembered as the king who brought a hundred-year-long conflict between the kingdoms of Avanti and Magadha to an end; he defeated Avanti and made it a territory of Magadha, that way further expanding the kingdom.

Shishunaga ruled until 395 BCE when he was succeeded by Kakavarna, also known as Kalashoka, who was Shishunaga's son. Kakavarna was the second king of the short-lived Shishunaga dynasty, which ended with Kakavarna's son and successor, Nandivardhan. Kakavarna divided the kingdom of Magadha between his ten sons, making his ninth son the heir to the throne.

Nandivardhan was killed by the Nandas, who took over Magadha and formed the Nanda Empire, subduing the Shishunaga dynasty by force and brutality around the mid-4th century BCE.

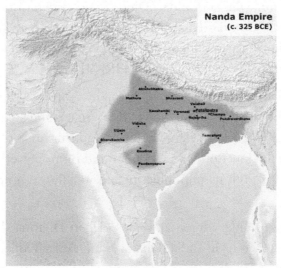

The Nanda Empire during its last ruler, Dhana Nanda, around 325 BCE. Credit: Wikimedia Commons.

According to ancient sources in India, Greece, and Rome, although the name of the Nanda dynasty's founder is unknown, the first king of the Nanda Empire was of low birth. The first king of the Nanda dynasty could have been a barber who got close to the queen and possibly became her lover. The sources credit the barber with good looks, charisma, and intelligence, which aided him in killing the king and later manipulating the queen into perceiving him as a guardian of the young princes who were to inherit their father's throne. After killing the princes, the barber founded the dynasty and became the first ruler of the Nanda Empire.

According to the Puranas, ancient Indian literature, the first ruler of the Nanda Empire and the founder of the Nanda dynasty was the son of the last Shishunaga king, Mahanandin, named Mahapadma Nanda. The name Mahapadma Nanda is translated as "lord of the great lotus."

Buddhist inscriptions, on the other hand, tell the tale of a thief and usurper who killed the last king of Shishunaga. He was later succeeded by his eight brothers, one of whom was the last king of the Nanda Empire, Dhana Nanda. There is no general quorum on the longevity of the Nanda dynasty and its wealthy empire; however, it is likely that the dynasty ended after the second generation of Nanda kings, so it probably spanned from 344 BCE to 321 BCE.

Dhana Nanda is translated as "Wealthy Nanda," which speaks in favor of all the riches that the Nanda dynasty accumulated during their short reign. The Nanda rulers were not popular among their subjects even though the kingdom was wealthier and more powerful than ever. The reason for both its unpopularity and wealth was a new system of taxation.

According to the tradition and tales of Jain Dharma (Jainism), one of the oldest religions in India, Dhana Nanda wasn't killed. Rather, he was allowed to leave the kingdom after he was defeated by Chandragupta Maurya, the founder of the Maurya Empire.

Although the lines between myth and fact are blurred when it comes to the Nanda Empire, it eventually ceased to exist, making room for the rise of a new force in ancient India: the Maurya Empire. However, between these two great empires, a new force was preparing to invade the territory of India. Before the Nandas would come to an end in 321 BCE, Alexander the Great would test his military skills and become one of the greatest generals in history.

Chapter 6 – The Invasion of Alexander the Great: The Aftermath of the Pan-Hellenic War

History rarely records such prolific rulers and military generals as Alexander the Great. By the age of thirty, Alexander the Great had more titles than almost any historical figure since the dawn of men. His titles included Basileus of Macedon, Hegemon of the Hellenic League, Strategos Autokrator of Greece, Shahanshah of Persia, Pharaoh of Egypt, and the Lord of Asia.

Alexander III of Macedon was born in 356 BCE and died at the young age of thirty-three in 323 BCE. However, before the end of his glorious days, Alexander the Great would almost become the ruler of the entire known ancient world thanks to his impeccable sense for military strategy and warfare.

Alexander belonged to an old dynasty of noblemen called the Argead. His father was King Philip II of Macedon, who was also an impressive ruler. Since Alexander was destined to rule, he had the finest education. His teacher was Aristotle, a famous polymath and philosopher who founded the Lyceum during the Classical period in ancient Greece.

Alexander inherited the throne when his father was murdered at the wedding of Cleopatra of Macedon in 336 BCE. Cleopatra was the only sibling of Alexander that shared the same parents.

The young king was only twenty years old at the time of his coronation. And in the first year of his rule, Alexander proved he had an extraordinary talent for warfare. He attacked and sacked Thebes, after which he was given the title of the general of Greece.

Two years before King Philip's unexpected and violent death, he had formed a coalition between all the Hellenic states except Sparta. This coalition was called the League of Corinth. This was the first time in the history of ancient Greece that all the Hellenic states managed to unify under a single central authority. Alexander assumed an important position in the league and was soon awarded the title Strategos Autokrator and Hegemon of the Hellenic League.

After proving to be worthy of his titles by smothering the rebellion of the allied states after his father's death, Alexander prepared for a military campaign that would be remembered as one of the greatest and boldest in the ancient world. Alexander was chosen to lead a campaign against the Persian Empire, also known as the Achaemenid Empire.

In 334 BCE, Alexander invaded Persia with a large force, starting a series of conquests and battles that would go on for an entire decade. Before defeating Persia and becoming a Shahanshah, Alexander the Great conquered Asia Minor, Syria, the Levant, Egypt, Babylonia, and Assyria. He was relentless and restless. Every goal Alexander achieved was a new way of surpassing himself.

In 326 BCE, only a year before the Nanda Empire would disintegrate, Alexander the Great fought King Porus after entering the Punjab region. This battle is known to history as the Battle of the Hydaspes.

After defeating Bessus of Bactria, one of the satraps (ministers) of Persia, in 328 BCE, Alexander decided to extend the Alexandrian Empire, which already stretched across Asia Minor and Persia. Before moving on to his next campaign, Alexander married an Iranian princess from Bactria, Roxana, which allowed him to strengthen his relationships with the satraps in Central Asia.

Alexander decided to invade India by crossing the Khyber Pass, located on the border between modern-day Pakistan and Afghanistan. Alexander left behind ten thousand men from his army to secure this area before marching through the Khyber Pass. Alexander and his men headed into Aornos and besieged the fortress that Heracles of myth failed to subdue. Alexander and his army were greatly outnumbered. They were attacked by Hindu clans from the Hindu Kush, which was west of the Himalayas. Still, Alexander the Great won and defeated the Hindu clans, even though it may have been the most difficult victory of all during his campaign east of the Persian Empire.

To penetrate deeper into the Indus Valley, Alexander would have to defeat Porus, who was a king in the Punjab region. If Alexander managed to conquer Porus, he would be the lord of Asia.

Alexander the Great and King Porus

After defeating the Hindu clans from the Hindu Kush, Alexander allied with King Taxiles, another king in the Punjab region. But Alexander faced resistance from King Porus, who ruled the stretch of territory from the Hydaspes (the Jhelum River) and Acesines (the Chenab River).

To face Porus's army and progress farther to the east while maintaining the loyalty of his Indian allies, Alexander needed to cross a monsoon-flooded river: the Hydaspes. Expecting Alexander and his army, Porus already lined some of his forces on the bank of the Hydaspes to prevent Alexander from crossing and getting closer to his capital. Alexander knew that rushing across the river with his entire contingent would mean doom for his troops. That is why he decided to move his army up and down the Hydaspes until he could find a suitable way to cross it.

When Alexander moved upstream, he found an uninhabited island that he could use to bring a part of his army to the other side of the river, which he did with no casualties being taken by the wild river streams.

Alexander ordered one of his generals, Craterus, to stay on the other side of the river with most of the men so that King Porus wouldn't find out about the crossing. If King Porus were to attack Alexander with all of his troops, Craterus was instructed to lead the greater part of the army across the river.

A painting depicting the Battle of the Hydaspes, Charles Le Brun, 17th century. Credit: Wikimedia Commons.

While Craterus waited on the other side of the river, Alexander ordered his military officers to cross the river at different locations. Alexander needed to make Porus believe that he was bluffing. Due to Alexander's heavy use of feint maneuvers, Porus eventually decided it was a bluff, which allowed Alexander and his men to cross the river unnoticed.

Porus was a worthy opponent, and as many historians note, the Battle of the Hydaspes was probably the most challenging conflict that Alexander had to endure to expand farther into India.

At one point, Porus saw through Alexander's intentions and knew that he would try to cross the river. He decided to send his son, also named Porus, to scout the area and report on Alexander's whereabouts. Luckily for Alexander, there was a major storm during the night of the crossing, so it was difficult for the young prince to spot any sign of Alexander. He and a part of his army used small vessels and animal skins filled with hay to get across the restless river.

After Alexander crossed the river, he decided to move the cavalry and archers to the front of the formation. Alexander's troops then faced Porus's son. Alexander ordered his foot archers to shower the younger Porus's army with arrows, after which the cavalry charged full force without a formation. They were followed by the phalanx. Porus's force was destroyed, and the young Porus had another problem as well—his chariot was stuck in the mud, as the soil was damped with water from the rain and storms.

The army at the river was destroyed, and Porus's son was among the casualties. King Porus was informed about the defeat and prepared to defend his territory with all of his forces, even equipping Indian war elephants. Every war elephant had a bed on its back, known as howdahs, that resembled miniature castles. At least three archers and another soldier with a javelin would be stationed on these beds.

Porus himself joined the battle, mounted on his biggest, strongest, and tallest war elephant. His soldiers were all dressed in vibrant clothes; they wore steel helmets and were equipped with maces and massive war axes.

Porus was in the very center of his army's formation, so Alexander decided to attack the cavalry from the right side to break the formation and reach Porus. He sent Dahae archers on horses to the right wing and the Macedon cavalry to the left. The Dahae were an Iranian people from Central Asia who entered into an alliance with Alexander. Alexander charged to the left wing with the Macedon cavalry, while General Coenus attacked from the back.

The Indian cavalry tried to defend themselves but entered into confusion, which resulted in Porus's cavalry fleeing behind the elephants to seek protection against Alexander's fierce attack.

Porus's war elephants brought a lot of damage to Alexander's army, as they tossed soldiers like ragdolls and pierced them with their tusks that were reinforced by steel. Alexander's infantry wasn't giving up or was even discouraged by the havoc that the elephants caused to their lines. They aimed for the elephant riders, known as mahouts. Whenever a mahout was struck down, his elephant would become disoriented, which helped the Macedonian army bring these massive beasts down.

The Indian cavalry didn't retreat, despite the chaos caused by some of the elephants. Instead, they charged at Alexander's cavalry. They were stopped by the foot soldiers, who were known as the pezhetairoi. The pezhetairoi used their shields to make a formation so they could push forward against the confused masses of Indian soldiers, that way aiding the Macedonian cavalry that was attacking from the back.

The Indian forces were already fleeing when Craterus managed to cross the river with the remaining forces kept at bay. Craterus arrived at the battlefield just at the right time to attack Porus's retreating soldiers.

Historians note that Alexander admired Porus when he realized that Porus would rather fight and die than get captured. Porus's military skill and valor appealed to young Alexander, who commanded his ally Taxiles to ask Porus to surrender. Taxiles went on a horse to convey Alexander's message, but Porus was nothing but infuriated once he saw his enemy riding toward him. He threw a spear at Taxiles, and Taxiles had no other choice but to flee. Alexander was determined to send his message, so he sent more messengers to Porus, only to have every one of them return with no success.

Finally, Porus's friend Meroes managed to convince the king to hear Alexander's message. Porus was already tired from battle. He was dehydrated and close to being defeated, so he dismounted his war elephant and asked for some water. Upon quenching his thirst, Porus agreed to be taken to Alexander.

When Alexander asked Porus how he wanted to be treated, Porus famously replied, "As a king would treat another king," probably meaning that he would rather be killed than captured and treated as a vassal or prisoner. Alexander was impressed by the king's reply, so he decided to treat him like the king he was. He decided to let Porus keep his territories and his power. Alexander founded two cities in Porus's territory: Alexandria Nicaea (to celebrate victory) and Bucephalus (Alexander's horse, who died after the battle).

Alexander's "Victory Coin" was minted in Babylon in 322 BCE, the year of Alexander's death. The coin depicts Alexander being crowned by the Hellenistic goddess of victory, Nike, and Alexander attacking Porus, who is mounted on a war elephant. Credit: Wikimedia Commons.

Alexander the Great and the Nanda Empire: Progressing to the East of India

Alexander fought what might be the greatest and most expensive battle in the history of Macedon. After allowing King Porus to keep his land and the privileges that come with being a king, Alexander decided to move farther to the east. Alexander arrived at the gates of the Nanda Empire, where he would face the last king of Nanda, Dhana Nanda.

Alexander might have won the battle against Porus, but the victory was bittersweet since Porus still did inflict havoc and devastation on Alexander's troops. Due to the numerous troubles that the Macedonian army had to overcome and put up with during the Battle of the Hydaspes, Alexander's army was discouraged, nearly begging their general, king, and leader—Alexander—to go back home instead of progressing farther to the east. Alexander's army wasn't involved in a mutiny in the core sense of the word; they weren't rebelling or threatening to leave their general. Rather, the Macedonian soldiers were convinced that they could not show any more fierceness than they did in the Battle of the Hydaspes. Moreover, many of them missed their families and were homesick. Moreover, the majority of Alexander's army in 326 BCE consisted of Persian forces. Still, Alexander decided to go on, arriving at the river Hyphasis, the modern-day Beas River, just outside the vast Nanda Empire.

Plutarch, the famous Greek philosopher and historian, tells a story about Alexander's desire to cross the Ganges and launch an attack on the Nanda Empire. In his book titled *Life of Alexander*, Plutarch includes details about Alexander's army defying him.

"As for the Macedonians, however, their struggle with Porus blunted their courage and stayed their further advance into India. For having had all they could do to repulse an enemy who mustered only twenty thousand infantry and two thousand horses, they violently opposed Alexander when he insisted on crossing the river Ganges also, the width of which, as they learned, was thirty-two furlongs, its depth a hundred fathoms, while its banks on the further side were covered with multitudes of men-at-arms and horsemen and elephants. For they were told that the kings of the Ganderites and Praesii were awaiting them with eighty thousand horsemen, two hundred thousand footmen, eight thousand chariots, and six thousand fighting elephants. And there was no boasting in these reports. For Androcottus, who reigned there not long afterwards, made a present to Seleucus of five hundred elephants, and with an army of six hundred thousand men overran and subdued all India."

Alexander's army was largely outnumbered, and they were all tired from the previous battle. It seems that the only man in the army of thousands who wanted to continue marching to the east was Alexander himself.

If the numbers recorded by Plutarch were accurate, Alexander had around forty thousand soldiers. But he was facing over 8,000 chariots, 6,000 war elephants, 200,000 infantry, and 80,000 cavalrymen; the odds were dramatically against the young king of Macedon. It is important to note that the Nanda Empire was extremely wealthy at the time, so these numbers very well could be true.

What Alexander failed to see in his ambition to conquer India and subdue the Nanda Empire was that entering deeper into India meant more dangerous jungles, unfamiliar terrain, and logistics and supply chain difficulties. Besides that, there were no ally forces on the other side of the Indus Valley on which Alexander could rely. All of these factors would make it difficult for Alexander to defeat any small kingdom in India. Nanda was an empire, meaning it was far from being small, weak, or poor.

When Alexander conquered the Persian Empire, it is important to note that the empire was already at its sunset. It had been weakened by a silent rebellion of viziers that were poisoning the rulers, and it was led by an inexperienced leader who came afterward, right at the time when Alexander was preparing his forces to take down the empire.

It is also important to note that compared to the Nanda Empire, Porus's kingdom was small. Porus was also "only" a king, whereas Dhana Nanda was an extremely wealthy emperor. If Porus gave Alexander and his army a hard time, conquering the Nanda Empire would be impossible, especially with an army of forty thousand soldiers.

After realizing that his soldiers opposed the planned attack on the Nanda Empire, Alexander decided that it was time to retreat and give up on his dreams of conquering the wealthy Nandas. Alexander, however, wasn't completely giving up on India, as he wanted to secure the borders of his empire. He moved his men south through Punjab and Sindh.

On his way south, Alexander and his army subdued several Hindu tribes living in the lower banks of the Indus River, which allowed him to secure the borders before turning to the west. Alexander returned to Babylon, where he resided in the palace of the late Nebuchadnezzar II, who died in 562 BCE.

Plutarch describes Alexander's days before his death, recording that the young conqueror spent time with Nearchus, one of Alexander's officers, and Medius of Larissa, also an officer and a personal friend of Alexander. They entertained themselves and drank wine for two days and nights, fourteen days before Alexander's untimely death. After two days of heavy drinking, Alexander became ill. He was so weak that he couldn't even speak; all he could do was lay in his bed. According to another ancient Greek historian, Diodorus, Alexander drank a massive bowl of wine to honor the great hero Heracles, after which he felt an immense pain that continued to plague him until his death ten days later. Diodorus also theorized that Alexander might have been poisoned, which would be logical given the fact that poisoning wasn't a strange way to get rid of a leader back then. Plutarch, however, disagrees with the theory of poisoning. Scholars today disagree over Alexander's cause of death.

Alexander had no heir. His son, who was named after him, was born to Roxana after his death. Thus, his closest officers and generals had to ask Alexander on his deathbed about his plans for the throne. According to an apocryphal story, Alexander said that he was leaving his empire "to the strongest," translated from the ancient Greek *tôi kratistôi*, which were supposedly his last words. It is argued that he said *tôi Kraterôi*, which would mean "to Craterus," who was his general and the regent of Macedon.

It is likely that Alexander couldn't even speak during his last days on Earth, for the illness or poison that struck him claimed his life in less than two weeks. This is what Plutarch records in his book about Alexander.

Diodorus, on the other hand, claims that Alexander chose Perdiccas, as Alexander gave him his signet ring. Diodorus even claims there were witnesses to confirm the story. Perdiccas was one of Alexander's faithful bodyguards and generals. Perdiccas supposedly wanted Alexander's and Roxana's unborn baby to become the new king if the child was male. Perdiccas, Craterus, Antipater, and Leonnatus would be the child's protectors.

In a way, the battle for power commenced, although perhaps in silence, when Meleager, one of Alexander's military officers, disagreed with the succession arranged by Perdiccas. Meleager instead decided to support Alexander's brother, Philip III Arrhidaeus. With the birth of Alexander's son, Alexander IV, the two sides set their differences aside and decided to support a shared rule between Alexander IV and Philip III.

This bust of Alexander the Great was made by Leochares around 330 BCE. It is located today in the Acropolis Museum in Athens. Credit: Wikimedia Commons.

After Alexander's death in 323 BCE, the Babylonian territories were divided among the satraps, and the battle for power commenced. Perdiccas was assassinated in 321 BCE, shortly after Alexander's death, and the forty-year-long war commenced between Alexander's successors, all of whom had claims to the throne of Macedonia and its territories won by Alexander the Great.

Once the four-decade war was settled, the Alexandrian Empire was divided into four pillars of power in the Hellenistic world: Ptolemaic Egypt, Attalid Anatolia, Seleucid Mesopotamia and Central Asia, and Antigonid Macedon.

Before his death, Alexander left detailed plans to Craterus, who presented them to Perdiccas. Perdiccas made sure that the Macedonians in Babylon heard the last plans of their now-dead leader. However, the Macedonians refused to conduct Alexander's plans, deeming them extravagant and unnecessary. According to Diodorus, Alexander wanted to invade the Mediterranean and Carthage with one thousand ships and unite people from Europe and Asia by mixing them through migrations to large settlements on the two continents. The plans further described the conquest of Arabia and building a monumental tomb for Alexander's father that would match the great pyramids of Egypt. None of Alexander's plans were conducted after his death. However, his legacy remains. Alexander the Great is still remembered as one of the greatest military generals, leaders, conquerors, and strategists in the history of war and men.

Shortly after Alexander's death, around 322 BCE, major changes were about to take place in India. The Nanda Empire was about to fall, making room for the rise of another great power: the Maurya Empire.

Chapter 7 – The Rise of the Maurya Empire

In 322 BCE, a new power ascended in the plains of the river Ganges.

The same empire that was once too big for Alexander and his army to take on was now under attack. And this battle would bring the king of the Nanda Empire, Dhana Nanda, to his knees.

According to a legend that draws roots from ancient Indian scriptures, Dhana Nanda, the ruler of the wealthy and vast Nanda Empire, offended Chanakya, a prominent Brahmin, in public. The Buddhist version of the legend says that Chanakya was born with canine teeth, which was considered to be a sign of royal origin. His mother feared that he would abandon her once he became king, so Chanakya broke his teeth to calm his mother. One day, Dhana Nanda organized a ceremony for Brahmins, which Chanakya attended. Once Dhana Nanda saw Chanakya, he was so disgusted and offended by his appearance—with his crooked legs, unsightly face, and broken teeth—that he ordered someone to remove Chanakya from the ceremony. Offended by the king's order, Chanakya promised to put an end to his reign and bring down his empire, which he did with his protégé, Chandragupta Maurya.

Another potential successor to the throne was Dhana Nanda's son, Pabbata, whom Chanakya convinced to seize the throne. To test who would be a better fit for the Nanda Empire, Chanakya gave an amulet on a thread to both Chandragupta and Pabbata. One night while Chandragupta was asleep, Chanakya asked Pabbata if he could take off Chandragupta's amulet without cutting the thread or waking him up. After Pabbata failed, Chanakya asked Chandragupta the next night if he could do the same. Chandragupta succeeded, so Chanakya chose him as the next king of the Nanda Empire.

There is little historical evidence to confirm any story wrapped in myth and legend, although it is known that Chanakya did help Chandragupta to become a king and the founder of a new empire. It is more likely that Chandragupta was advised and taught by Chanakya, who utilized the power vacuum that was formed after the death of Alexander the Great. Around 323 BCE, Alexander's empire in Asia was divided into regions and pieced into various satraps in the Greater Punjab area, so Chandragupta decided to conquer and subdue Greek satraps in South Asia, knowing that it would pave the way to conquering the Nanda Empire.

Perhaps the reason there are so many legends surrounding the conquest of the Nanda Empire is that there are few details in Indian scriptures about the end of Nanda or Dhana Nanda that could be fact. What is known is that Chandragupta was of unknown origin, while his ancestors remain a secret hidden in the ancient past.

The majority of written sources on the conquest of the Nanda Empire were written at least two hundred years after Chandragupta had formed one of the biggest empires in ancient India. Plutarch also wrote about Chandragupta, the decline of Nanda, and the rise of the Mauryan Empire. As Plutarch writes, young Chandragupta might have met Alexander the Great when he was still a teenager at Taxiles's court, where he was taught by his guru, Chanakya. Maybe Chandragupta saw Alexander as the personification of a universal emperor; after all, he had a dream to become one himself, which he later did in his early twenties by forming the Maurya Empire. Many historians argue that Chandragupta might have met Alexander, but there is no factual proof that their encounter ever happened.

According to various Latin, Hellenistic, and Indian sources, Chandragupta was determined to bring the Nanda Empire down so he could subdue all of South Asia and establish a firm hold over the Indo-Gangetic Plain. Chandragupta Maurya commenced his conquest by first subduing and raiding the surrounding settlements, villages, and regions. Afterward, Chandragupta hired Hindu mercenaries and decided to go for the center of power in the Nanda Empire, targeting the capital of Pataliputra. There, he killed his father, and the rest is, well, history.

Chanakya played an important role in these conquests, as he taught Chandragupta everything he knew about politics, making alliances, wars, and statesmanship. After conquering the Nanda Empire, Chandragupta founded a new empire in 321 BCE while securing the borders to the west and continuing with his expansion politics.

Chandragupta the Unifier, Chanakya, and the Maurya Empire: Politics, Organization, and Management

One of the greatest legacies of Chanakya, also known as Kautilya in many ancient sources, was the *Arthashastra*. The *Arthashastra* is an ancient scripture about politics, statecraft, economy, and military strategy that contains important lessons and collected knowledge Chanakya had imparted to Chandragupta. Chandragupta used the *Arthashastra* to manage and organize his empire, which was the largest central power that had been known at this point in India.

Chanakya placed a major emphasis on recruiting spies in the name of the king so that the ruler would always be aware of what was being talked about among his courtiers, subjects, and neighboring kingdoms. The logistics of running a network of spies is described in the book in detail, and it includes background checks and the screening of ministers.

The name of the book, *Arthashastra*, can be translated as "the science of wealth" or even "science of political economy." The treatise touches on many subjects, though, such as the market and trading, economy, law, ethics, and war theories. It also explores the subject of nature, peace, medicine, animals, agriculture, and diplomacy. The book includes strategies for questions of social welfare, advising the king about actions he should take in case of famine, natural disasters, and other cases of misfortune. For example, in case a natural disaster strikes or the empire is affected by famine, the king should absolve those who are affected from paying taxes. Moreover, the king should start a public project, which would show the people that their leader was still in control and very much potent. Public projects could be building forts, aqueducts, irrigation systems, or similar constructions that would keep any chaos or mutiny at bay amidst crises.

After the Maurya Empire was founded, Chanakya naturally became Chandragupta's chief minister. With the help and guidance of Chanakya, Chandragupta captured numerous Indian territories from Greek satraps who were appointed after Alexander the Great's death. Chandragupta even killed some of the satraps to show his dominance over the Indo-Gangetic Plain. By 317 BCE, all the Macedonian satraps had been removed from Indian territories or executed by the king of Maurya.

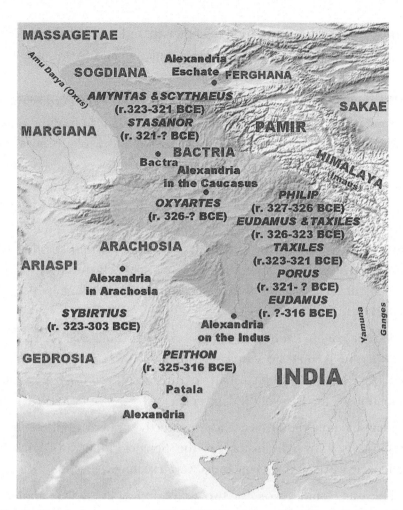

The Indian subcontinent, 317 BCE. By this point, Chandragupta had wrested the Indian territories from the Macedonian satraps. Credit: Wikimedia Commons.

Five years later, in 312 BCE, Seleucus I Nicator came on the political scene of ancient India. He posed a threat to Chandragupta's Maurya Empire, as his newly founded kingdom was facing the empire from its eastern border. Nicator was already familiar with the terrain of the Indian subcontinent, having been one of the generals of Alexander the Great. He was also one of many friends, family members, and generals who fought over the throne of the Alexandrian Empire. A decade after Alexander's death, Nicator formed a new Hellenistic power center in India called the Seleucid Empire. The empire stretched to Mesopotamia and Syria, also taking most of Asia Minor and the Iranian Plateau.

For a bit of background, Nicator gave his support to Perdiccas after Alexander's death in 323 BCE. However, after a mutiny against Perdiccas erupted due to his failure to subdue Ptolemy in Egypt, Nicator conspired with two other generals, Antigenes and Peithon. They killed Perdiccas in 321 BCE. While Antipater (one of Alexander's generals) became the regent of the Macedonian kingdom, Nicator was given the title of Babylonian satrap. However, the shift of power swiftly changed the situation, as Antigonus, perhaps the most powerful Macedonian general at the time, claimed the throne as the new regent, and Nicator didn't have many options but to flee and leave Babylon.

Nicator couldn't return to his power center until 312 BCE, which was when he formed his empire in South Asia. He gradually took the title of Chiliarch, Shahanshah of Persia, Lord of Asia, and, pretentiously, the King of the Universe.

Chandragupta didn't face Nicator directly in a war until 305 BCE. This war is known to history as the Seleucid-Mauryan War. The Hellenistic world and ancient India were clashing yet again.

The war would go on for two years, but sadly, details about the Seleucid-Mauryan War are scarce. What is known to history is that Nicator wanted to win over the remaining satraps who once belonged to the Macedonians. At one point during the war, Nicator crossed the river Indus. It is not clear where the first battle of the war took place due to the lack of information, but it is certain that Seleucus I Nicator faced a wild river with a hostile empire waiting on the other side.

The war ended in 303 BCE with a treaty between the Mauryan Empire and the Seleucid Empire. The treaty was also strengthened with a political marriage. Seleucus gave the hand of his daughter, Helena, to Chandragupta, which allowed Helena to become a Mauryan princess. However, the mother of the king's successor wasn't

Helena; that honor belonged to Durdhara. Chandragupta had another wife, as polygamy was customary and a part of the monarchial tradition in ancient India. There are no details on the lineage of Durdhara or her life, except for the information that Durdhara gave birth to the heir of the throne, Bindusara.

Along with giving his daughter's hand to Chandragupta, Seleucus Nicator also gave up the provinces in the far east of his empire. In return, Chandragupta became his ally and gave him five hundred war elephants, which would help Seleucus in his long war between Alexander's generals and family members who were fighting over his territories.

Chandragupta continued his expansionist politics after 302 BCE, as he now had a valuable ally keeping the borders between the two empires stable and secure. The Mauryan king extended his empire to the southern parts of India and the Deccan Plateau.

When almost the entire Indian subcontinent was unified, Chandragupta and his chief minister Chanakya began making reforms in politics and the economy. Chandragupta created a strong central authority, which resided in the capital of his empire, Pataliputra. He ruled with a council of ministers, with Chanakya, of course, acting as the chief minister. This central authority ruled over the entire empire, which was divided into janapadas (territories). Each territory was protected and secured with forts.

The administration was layered, as Chandragupta employed tax collectors, spies, jurors, councilors, and even law officers, which would have been similar to modern-day police officers. Chandragupta's law officers were supposed to keep law and order across the empire; this is why the crime rate was extremely low. The empire also had an administration for agriculture, cities, and the military. Each worked simultaneously to keep the empire running smoothly.

In the religious realm, Chandragupta frequently organized sacrifices following Vedic tradition and Brahmin rituals. He also planned religious festivals, which would include processions with horses and elephants throughout the capital.

Chandragupta would rarely leave the palace. Chanakya was aware of the dangers of being king, and he knew that potential assassins could try to kill Chandragupta. To keep the king safe, Chanakya created strategies to protect him. Chandragupta was allowed to publicly attend sacrifices and ritual ceremonies. He could also leave the safety of his court for important government business and war campaigns. Chandragupta would often change his bedroom, which was supposed to set possible assassins off the king's trail. Chanakya even made sure to keep Chandragupta safe from court conspiracies; whenever the king would go on a hunting trip, he would be sent with a special unit comprised of all-female guards. Female guards were considered less likely to engage in court intrigue. When Chandragupta would attend a religious ceremony, though, he would be surrounded by male guards.

The king's safety was a top priority, but so was the economy of the Maurya Empire. Chandragupta built numerous water tanks, irrigation systems, temples, and roads to ensure that the entire population could get food and other supplies. The king also used these roads to send supplies to the forces that were far from home. This practice would become one of Chandragupta's many legacies, as other successors to the throne would consider it a standard.

The empire depended greatly on trading, and Chandragupta created trading networks, manufacturing centers, and wider roads that were more suitable for transporting goods in carts. There is evidence of multiple miles-long highways leading in and out of the empire to Nepal, Taxila, Dehradun, Odisha, Mirzapur, Kapilavastu, Karnataka, and Andhra. The capital of Pataliputra and Taxila were directly connected with a thousand-mile-long highway, which was used for commerce, travel, and postal transportation. The highway was known as Uttarapatha.

It is somewhat peculiar that there is not much evidence of art and elaborate architecture in the Maurya Empire. Archaeologists have not been able to find many remains of art except for scriptures that were mostly written by Chanakya and Megasthenes. Megasthenes was a Greek historian and an ambassador of Seleucus I Nicator. He lived at Chandragupta's court, serving as an Indian ethnographer. Megasthenes wrote a book about his exploration of India called *Indica* (also referred to as *Indika*). The original scripture is lost; however, some fragments were retrieved by archaeologists.

The Abdication and Death of Chandragupta

Chandragupta's son, Bindusara, was coronated in 297 BCE, which is the year that historians take as the year of Chandragupta's abdication. It wasn't unusual for monarchs of ancient India to abdicate the throne and let their successor rule in their stead. If that happened, it was customary for the abdicated king to turn to an ascetic way of life, which was the case for Chandragupta's abdication as well.

There is not much evidence as to why Chandragupta decided it was time for him to step down after ruling for twenty-four years. According to a legend that is deeply rooted in Jainism, which was Chandragupta's religion, the king had sixteen dreams that brought nightmares during his days. He dreamed of a famine that would last for twelve years, the morale of his people decreasing, and the loss of strategically and historically important territories. All of this havoc would be brought to Maurya because of the violence Chandragupta had inflicted during his conquests.

So, according to Jain tradition, after having these dreams and wishing to redeem for his past as an imperialistic conqueror, Chandragupta decided to abdicate and make his son, Bindusara, the king to the vast Maurya Empire. There are little to no records of Chandragupta's days as an ascetic monk, but it is known that

Chandragupta died during meditation. At the time, he was ritually starving himself to death, a practice known as Sallekhana.

Perhaps the greatest monument to Jainism from the first years of the Maurya Empire is the Chandragupta basadi, which was built in honor of Chandragupta. A basadi is a Jain temple, and it is similar in style to Hindu and ancient Buddhist temples. The Chandragupta basadi is located on Chandragiri Hill in the Indian state of Karnataka.

The Chandragupta basadi, supposedly built by Chandragupta Maurya and located on Chandragiri Hill. Credit: Wikimedia Commons.

Chandragupta is still remembered as the great unifier of Indian states and kingdoms, as well as the founder of one of the largest and most powerful empires ever established in the Indian subcontinent.

Chapter 8 – The Maurya Dynasty and Life in the Maurya Empire

It is believed that Chandragupta abdicated in favor of his son Bindusara in 297 BCE. There is not much detail on Bindusara's life, as most of the information that is known about the second king of Maurya comes from sources written a thousand years after Bindusara's rule. Other sources related to Bindusara are mostly veiled in legends and myths. Bindusara was overshadowed by his father's fame and later by his son's achievements, which probably did not help matters either.

Bindusara: "The Strength of the Drop"

Even though Durdhara is considered to be Bindusara's mother according to the Jain tradition, there is a possibility that Bindusara is half Greek Macedonian, as his mother might have been Helena of Seleucus. However, there is no proof that would testify in favor of this theory, as the only source that talks about Bindusara's origins claim that Durdhara is his mother.

One of the most famous legends about Bindusara talks about how the young prince got his name. Chanakya, Chandragupta's chief minister and guru, used to take great care in protecting his king against potential poisoning, knowing that conspiracies could often put an end to a king's life. That is why Chanakya used to put small doses of various poisons in Chandragupta's food. One day, while the king's wife, Durdhara, was pregnant, the king decided to share his meal with his wife, not knowing that his portion contained poison. The queen was only seven days from the predicted day of delivery. As she ate a morsel that had poison in it, Chanakya realized that the queen was going to die in moments. Durdhara collapsed, already dying in front of her husband, and Chanakya shared what had happened and offered to save the baby while he still could.

He decapitated the dead queen with a sword and cut her womb open to get the baby out. He noticed that a drop of poison had touched the baby's head. This is how Bindusara got his name. When translated from Sanskrit, bindu means "drop." Bindusara as a whole means "the strength of the drop."

To keep the baby alive until he was supposed to be born, Chanakya ordered a goat to be killed and cut open so he could place the baby inside. After seven days, Bindusara was born again.

Bindusara ruled from the abdication of his father in 297 BCE to either 272 BCE or 270 BCE. Taranatha, a Tibetan historian who lived between the 16th and 17th centuries, wrote about Bindusara's conquest hundreds of years later. Taranatha writes that Chanakya defeated sixteen lords in the surrounding territories of the Maurya Empire, which extended the empire's borders to the Bay of Bengal and the Arabian Sea. However, many historians argue that it was his father, Chandragupta, who conquered these territories and that Bindusara only retained them.

Bindusara had three sons: Sushima, Ashoka, and Vigatashoka. According to legend, though, Bindusara had 101 sons and 16 wives; of course, it is highly unlikely he fathered so many children. Ashoka and Vigatashoka are said to have been born by the same mother. According to the Indian scripture about Ashoka, the *Ashokavadana*, Bindusara didn't like Ashoka, as Ashoka had limbs that were "hard to the touch."

This text states that Ashoka's mother was Subhadrangi, also known as Damma or Dharma. She was of modest origin but had a Brahmin background. She was so beautiful that all the other king's wives became instantly jealous of her. When Subhadrangi's father presented her to the king, Bindusara was astonished, but his wives insisted that he keep her as a royal barber.

Bindusara was impressed by her skills as a hairdresser, but he was even more impressed with her beauty. After Bindusara learned that she had a Brahmin background (he was a follower of Brahminism himself), he decided to make her his wife.

As the *Mahavamsa* (a chronicle of Sri Lanka) tells it, Ashoka wasn't supposed to inherit the throne. In fact, King Bindusara had appointed his eldest son, Sushima, to be his successor. According to one of many legends covering the circumstances around the succession of the empire, Ashoka was appointed as the viceroy of Ujjain. Once he heard of his father's death, he rushed back to the capital of Pataliputra and killed ninety-nine of his brothers, including the eldest, leaving only the brother with whom he shared the same mother.

Another story suggests that Sushima was, once again, the favorite son and proclaimed heir of Bindusara. Sushima liked to show his dominance among the court officials and king's ministers. On one occasion, he threw a weapon at one of the ministers, whose name was Khallataka. Khallataka was so enraged by Sushima's outburst that he deemed him unfit to be the king and demanded the royal council of five hundred to vote and appoint Ashoka as the new emperor.

The major twist in the story was that Khallataka also shared with the council that Ashoka was predicted to be a great universal emperor. This was apparently a premonition by the devatas, female and male spirits that represent the counterparts of someone's soul according to many religions originating from India.

Bindusara was still alive, though, and he wanted to abdicate and let his eldest son rule the empire. When the council shared its decision to appoint Ashoka as the new emperor, Bindusara wasn't happy with their choice, as he wanted Ashoka to become the governor of Takshashila. While Bindusara was arguing that Ashoka shouldn't be the emperor, he died. However, he was alive long enough to witness the devatas appearing in front of him, as if by miracle, and coronating Ashoka as the new king.

Once Sushima heard the news, he rushed to the capital of Pataliputra from Takshashila, where the council had sent him. He intended to claim his right to the throne.

However, Radhagupta, Khallataka's son, tricked Sushima and stopped him from getting to the royal palace. Instead, Radhagupta sent him to a pit of burning coal, where he died. Ashoka became the third emperor of the great Maurya Empire, and he would become just as famous as his grandfather, Chandragupta, in the years to come.

As far as Bindusara's death, he might have died around 270 BCE, while other historians suggest that he died in 272 BCE.

Ashoka the Great: "Beloved of the Gods"

Ashoka, also known as Ashoka the Great, is one of the most celebrated monarchs in the history of India. He was coronated in 268 BCE and ruled until 232 BCE. When translated from Sanskrit, the name Ashoka means "without sorrow." The legend from the *Ashokavadana* notes that he was given the name by his mother, whose sorrows were all swept away when he was born.

Ashoka also had the royal name Priyadasi, meaning "a man of grace," as well as the title of Devanampriya Piyadasi, which translated from Sanskrit means "beloved of the gods" or "the one who treats people kindly." What is interesting about the name, life, and character of Ashoka is that he was completely unknown to history until a British historian named James Prinsep discovered evidence of his existence in 1837, more than two thousand years after Ashoka's death. Once Ashoka was identified, he was soon attested as one of the greatest monarchs in the history of ancient India and beyond.

Devanampriya Piyadasi, one of Ashoka's titles, found on the Lumbini pillar. Credit: Wikimedia Commons.

Ashoka wasn't always regarded as "humane" and "kind," even though some of his titles imply this. According to Taranatha, at the beginning of Ashoka's reign, he was known as Kamashoka, which roughly translated means "the one who seeks pleasure." Later, he was called Chandashoka, which means "Ashoka the fierce," as he performed several cruel acts. One such cruel deed was described in the legends of Ashoka. After Ashoka ascended the throne, he wanted to test his ministers' loyalty to him. He ordered them to cut every plant and tree bearing fruit or flower. When the ministers failed to complete the task, he decapitated all five hundred of them.

Although the story is exaggerated, as is often the case with legends and myths, there are many stories that testify to Ashoka's cruelty. One of these stories involves Radhagupta, who became Ashoka's prime minister. Radhagupta wanted to keep the king unsullied by all the killings he had committed since he was coronated, so he decided to find someone who would do these deeds for the king. Radhagupta found a boy who was later known as Chandagirika, meaning "Girika the fierce," who tortured and killed people instead of the king. Ashoka supposedly ordered his men to build a prison that had a marvelous exterior but held blood and gore within its pretty walls.

All of these stories of Ashoka's cruel deeds might be an exaggeration. By doing this, writers could present Buddhism as a transforming and noble religion that managed to change Ashoka's evil ways and convert him into a kind man and beloved king.

But before Ashoka's conversion to Buddhism, the king was focused on warfare and conquests. He had his sights set on the flourishing kingdom of Kalinga.

Ashoka pillar found in Vaishali, Bihar, India, built by King Ashoka of Maurya around 250 BCE. Credit: Wikimedia Commons.

Kalinga was once a part of the Nanda Empire, but it gained its autonomy with the fall of the empire in 321 BCE, which was also the time when the Maurya Empire was founded. Kalinga had an elaborate art milieu, and the people of Kalinga were known for being a peaceful nation. They had no conflicts with other states, and no war campaigns were led by their king, Mahodadhi Pati, which is translated as "the lord of the seas." This was a suitable title for the Kalinga king, given the fact that the kingdom had a strong and well-equipped navy.

What bothered Ashoka was the fact that the Kalinga king had an elaborate network of trading outposts and that he controlled the coastline since the kingdom was connected to the Bay of Bengal. With such a network, the Kalinga king, if he so willed, could cut communication between the capital of Maurya and the rest of central India. Thus, Ashoka prepared for a war campaign that would lead to the start of the Kalinga War in 261 BCE, around seven years after Ashoka came to the throne.

Before attacking and leading his military toward the Kalinga kingdom, Ashoka sent a message to the king, demanding him to submit to the Maurya Empire. The king didn't want to bow to Ashoka, which meant only one thing to Ashoka: war.

Ashoka was determined to win the war against Kalinga since it would be his first major conquest. So, he brought a large army equipped with the very best weaponry that Maurya had at its disposal. The Maurya Empire was vast and wealthy, and all the odds spoke in favor of Ashoka winning the war. However, the people of Kalinga cherished their independence so much that they put up a strong and vigorous defense.

The people of Kalinga showed their fierceness in the fight to defend their autonomy and the borders of their kingdom. Ashoka's determination to win and subdue Kalinga took over 250,000 lives on both sides. Many people of Kalinga died from wounds soon after the war, so the casualties were even greater than that. As far as the 250,000 casualties go, the Kalinga War is so far the deadliest in Indian history.

Ashoka was forced to face the horrors he had wrought. Children wandered alone, trying to find the bodies of their dead parents. Crippled soldiers attempted to drag themselves from the field of battle, while widows desperately looked for their husbands' bodies. It all came crashing down on Ashoka, and he started to blame himself for it all. Even though Maurya had won, the king of Maurya felt like he had lost.

He decided to take a path of nonviolence and turned to Buddhism, which meant that all war campaigns ceased at once. The remaining days of Ashoka's rule were filled with peace and prosperity. Harmony would prevail in the Maurya Empire for nearly four decades.

According to Buddhist tradition, during his reign, Ashoka built over eighty-four thousand Buddhist temples and monasteries. The number of temples is a product of exaggeration; scholars claim that later inscriptions attributed old temples and monasteries to Ashoka in an attempt to show his devotion to Buddhism. The Buddhist tradition also tells a story of Ashoka finding and collecting most of the relics of Gautama Buddha, which he kept in the temples and monasteries.

The Great Stupa of Sanchi is attributed to King Ashoka. It is a UNESCO World Heritage Site today. Credit: Biswarup Ganguly, Wikimedia Commons.

Ashoka's edicts speak in favor of his path to Buddhism and Dharma (Dhamma). These were written on pillars, caves, and boulders across the Maurya Empire and Indian subcontinent. There are Major and Minor Edicts, which were divided, deciphered, and categorized by historian James Prinsep. The first edicts were written on stones, probably around the tenth year of Ashoka's rule. One such edict is positioned at the border with the Hellenistic kingdoms and territories in India, and the inscription on the stone testifies that it might have been created at least two years after Ashoka returned from Kalinga.

Major Pillar Edict, inscription on a column, Bihar, India. Credit: Sachin Kumar Tiwary, Wikimedia Commons.

The edicts were made by Ashoka and spoke about Buddhism, Buddha, Dharma, and Ashoka himself. The main purpose of these pillars and stones was to bring these teachings to a wider audience. These edicts were meant to be seen by everyone, and they preached about morality, kindness, generosity, and other virtues that would pass the spirit of Buddhism.

Many of Ashoka's edicts tell stories about the king's generosity and kindness and all the ways he took care of his subjects, human and animal alike. Ashoka is presented as a person who had a change of heart. He had kindness not only for the people of Maurya but also for the people beyond his borders. Ashoka supposedly even shared medical treatments and knowledge with other kingdoms and regions and generally cared about the welfare of all people.

Ashoka would send officers to check on the welfare of the people and respond to their needs. These officers were known as Mahamatras, which means "officers of the faith." Ashoka's edicts state that these officers were anointed by the king himself to advocate for morality and help others who were suffering.

Another significant edict was found in Lumbini, Nepal, the supposed birthplace of Buddha. As the edict proclaims, King Ashoka came to Lumbini two decades after his conversion to Buddhism and his famous change of heart. He erected a pillar bearing an edict about Buddha's birth to mark the spot where the Blessed One, as he addresses Buddha, began his life on Earth. To bless the people of Lumbini, Ashoka exempted them from taxes and asked only for an eighth of their yearly crops.

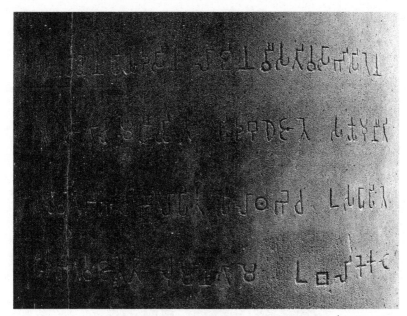

The Pillar Edict in Lumbini, the birthplace of Buddha, was erected by Ashoka twenty years after the Kalinga War. Credit: Wikimedia Commons.

The Kalsi rock edict tells a story about Ashoka's new conquests, conquests that were not achieved by steel and armies but rather with Dharma and the path to enlightenment. The Kalsi rock inscription, located in Dehradun District, mentions Greek kings, including Alexander of Epirus, Antigonus Gonatas of Macedon, Ptolemy II of Egypt, Magas of Cyrene, and Antiochus II Theos of Syria. Officers of the Buddhist faith were sent to their kingdoms as ambassadors. Whether these ambassadors were received by the Hellenistic kings is not mentioned in the edict. However, it is certain that ancient Greek philosophers presented Indian thought and philosophy to contemporary thinkers and polymaths.

Excavation of the Lumbini pillar, revealing the inscription at the bottom, 1896, Alois Anton Führer, British Library. Credit: Wikimedia Commons.

Despite Ashoka's efforts and monumental endeavors to implement Buddhism in the Maurya Empire and beyond to the Greek states and kingdoms, he didn't manage to convert even a majority of his population. Most of the people inhabiting the Mauryan Empire weren't Buddhists, and they weren't willing to convert to Buddhism.

The *Arthashastra* says a strong kingdom can only be ruled by a strong king. A strong king needs to consider what is in the best interest of the majority of his people and should not indulge in his own desires. Ashoka wanted to maintain the image of a strong king according to this philosophy, so he wouldn't implement Buddhism as the state religion. Ashoka's emissaries spread his decree that everyone's religion should be respected and that no man should place his religion over someone else's. This thought perfectly illustrated the religious milieu in the Maurya Empire, as there were religious clans of Zoroastrianism, Hinduism, Jainism, Ajivikism, Greek polytheism, and Buddhism.

However, despite the image of peace and kindness, Ashoka was still fierce even after his conversion to Buddhism. According to the *Ashokavadana*, he is said to have tortured Chandagirika to death in his prison, which was called Ashoka's Hell. You might recall that Chandagirika was Ashoka's chief executioner who tortured people in the king's stead, but he eventually became the victim due to his cruel ways. Ashoka also punished sixteen thousand heretics, slaying them for the misconduct of only one non-Buddhist who drew Buddha bowing to another deity. Still, many scholars argue that these stories are a figment of imagination made by rivaling religious cults who wanted to show Ashoka as a cruel and immoral ruler.

Ashoka's pillar in Vaishali, Bihar, India. Credit: Wikimedia Commons.

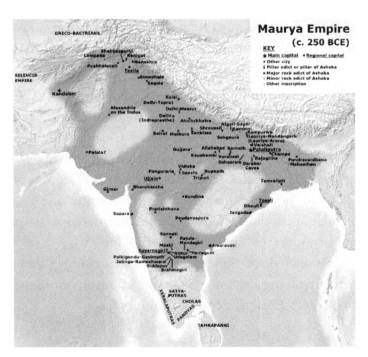

The largest extent of the Maurya Empire during Ashoka's reign, around 250 BCE. Credit: Wikimedia Commons.

Ashoka's death was not mentioned in any of the edicts, but the last edict was erected in his twenty-sixth regnal year.

After ruling for nearly forty years, Ashoka died, leaving the throne to his grandson, as none of his sons could ascend the throne in his stead. His son Kunala was blind, another son named Mahendra was spreading Buddhism across the empire and beyond, and there is not much information about Jalauka. Ashoka's favorite son, Tivala, who was the father of Ashoka's successor, Dasharatha, died before Ashoka.

The only story concerning Ashoka's death is found in the Sri Lankan tradition, claiming that the king died in 232 BCE. According to the story, Ashoka became very ill, and he started donating funds from the empire's treasury until his ministers prohibited donations to the sanghas and monks. The king then began to donate his possessions. Royal ministers had to find a way to prevent him from doing this. Dying and ill, Ashoka only had half of a myrobalan fruit left, which he gave to monks as his final donation.

Myrobalan fruit, Phyllanthus emblica. *Credit: Prathyush Thomas.*

The story of Ashoka's last days is considered a fabrication to show Ashoka in the best possible light and to emphasize the importance of giving.

After Ashoka's prosperous reign, which lasted for almost four decades, the kingdom slowly began its decline. The great and vast Maurya Empire would fall in the next fifty years, and with it, Ashoka's pillars and legacy would be buried in the sand for centuries.

Dasharatha and the Last Kings of Maurya

Dasharatha inherited the throne from his grandfather in 232 BCE, and he tried to follow his grandfather's steps and continue his legacy. Dasharatha attempted to keep the empire together after Ashoka's death, but his efforts were in vain.

The first one to interrupt the political unity of the Maurya Empire was Dasharatha's uncle, Jalauka. Jalauka founded an independent kingdom in Kashmir, located in the northwest of the Indian subcontinent. Some historians point out that Dasharatha already shared the throne of the Maurya Empire with Kunala, thus dividing the empire. Dasharatha also started to lose provinces in the northwest, while one of the nobles, Virasena, became the self-proclaimed king of Gandhara, one of the long-disestablished sixteen Mahajanapadas. Kalinga also departed from the empire, while some of Dasharatha's governors sought autonomy for their appointed territories and regions.

The empire was steadily losing its territorial vastness, and the new king of Maurya was losing his political relevance in the wider region of the Indian subcontinent.

Dasharatha was succeeded by Kunala's son, Samprati, in 224 BCE. Samprati was born and raised in the region of Ujjain, where Ashoka had once been appointed as a governor. Ashoka was still alive when Kunala came with Samprati to Pataliputra to claim his right to the throne. Ashoka supposedly replied that he couldn't make Kunala the king because he was blind. According to some sources, particularly in Jain tradition, Kunala was not born blind; he had been blinded as a result of a cruel conspiracy to rob him of his right to the throne. Regardless, Ashoka promised that Samprati would become the king after Dasharatha.

Samprati proved to be another great Mauryan monarch, as he managed to retrieve some of the provinces that had departed during Dasharatha's reign.

Unlike his grandfather Ashoka, Samprati spread the word and influence of Jainism across the empire. The Jain tradition credit Samprati as the patron of Jain monks, and he is also credited for rebuilding numerous temples and erecting statues of idols across the Maurya Empire.

Samprati was succeeded by his son, Shalishuka, who reigned from 215 BCE to 202 BCE. A Puranic Sanskrit text mentions Shalishuka as an unforgiving and unrighteous ruler, but not much is known about him and his regnal years. The relationship between Shalishuka and his successor Devavarman is not completely clear, although it is likely that they were father and son. Devavarman isn't described as cruel or unrighteous, but he is attributed with weakness during his seven years of ruling.

Devavarman was succeeded by Shatadhanvan in 195 BCE, who ruled until 187 BCE when he was succeeded by Brihadratha.

Brihadratha would be the last king of the Maurya Empire, and he ruled for three brief years. Puranic sources claim that the last king of Maurya ruled for seven years, ending his reign in 180 BCE.

Brihadratha was killed in a conspiracy set by his general, Pushyamitra Shunga, in 184 BCE. An Indian poet from the 7th century named Banabhatta writes that Pushyamitra wanted to show the king the extent of his army. While the army was marching in all its glory, Pushyamitra killed the king in front of everyone and claimed the throne. Pushyamitra Shunga then founded a new ruling dynasty that would control Magadha.

The Indian subcontinent would never see another empire that could compare to the vastness and power of the Maurya Empire.

Chapter 9 – Life in Ancient India: The People of India from the Indus Valley Civilization to the Maurya Empire

Amidst great wars, conquests, and battles for power, the average person in ancient India lived fairly mundane lives. But how did the people of India live at the very beginning of the Indus Valley civilization, and how did their lifestyle change with migrations, conquests, Alexander the Great, and the Maurya Empire?

Everyday Life of the Indus Valley Civilization

Like many people of the ancient world who lived in a hot climate, the people of the Indus Valley spent a lot of their time outside since most of them lived in small, cramped houses. Even though these homes were small and often served as a working space as well, the rooftops were flat. This allowed the ancient people of the Indus Valley to use their roofs as an extra space to sleep, especially during extremely hot nights.

Wealthier people had courtyards, where they could plant flowerbeds or some fruit and vegetables to add to the table. They also used their courtyards to relax.

It is not certain whether all children went to school, but children did help around with daily chores. Children were taught to hunt, craft, cook, and farm. Hard work wasn't the only thing in these children's lives; they also had time to play. Scholars believe that both adults and children liked board games and dice games since dice with holes similar to the ones we use today have been found in numerous excavations over the years. Some historians think that the first dice could have been invented in ancient India. Children also played with whistles that often were shaped into different animals and birds. Another popular toy for children was terracotta monkeys that would roll by pulling a long string. Archaeologists have also discovered carts, and it is thought that children ran alongside the carts as they rolled down the hill or just observed the cart rolling down.

Most of the population at the time were either craftsmen, artisans, farmers, or hunters. But regardless of one's occupation, everyone depended on the Indus for life. From agricultural settlements on the banks of the river Indus to great cultural centers like Harappa, the fertile lands of the river were the ticking vein of a strong civilization. There was food in abundance, as agriculture developed at a fast pace, with elaborate irrigation and water storage systems. This allowed people to focus on other things besides work. Adults could swim in public pools, refresh, and take care of their hygiene.

Dancing was also an important part of religion, culture, and entertainment. Excavated figurines of dancing women can testify to this. People would also attend religious ceremonies and festivals a few times a year, which was also a way of socializing and sharing spiritual beliefs.

The people of ancient India could differentiate economic class based on the houses they lived in, but one could also tell societal differences based on clothing. The more colorful and more layered the robes were, the wealthier the person. Wealthy women would also wear a lot of gold jewelry with precious gems to show off their economic status.

Whether you were wealthy or not, your day would begin with breakfast. People in ancient India had three meals a day, just as we do in modern times. For breakfast, they would often eat wheat or porridge with dates. Hydration was also important, especially during the hot days of summer, so water almost always accompanied breakfast. For lunch, they would have something refreshing, like melon, grapes, or other fruit that grew in the Indus Valley. For dinner, they would eat barley, peas, and wine, while the wealthy would also have meat. The poor who had learned to hunt also might have meat for dinner, or they would sell it.

Traders probably relied on bartering, as the Indus Valley civilization didn't mint coins. Archaeologists once found thousands of small rectangular tablets, which they thought were a form of coins or money. However, it was later determined that these were stamps; they were probably used by traders to create tags for their merchandise.

As smaller settlements turned into urbanized centers and cities, the life of the ancient Indus people changed with it.

Everyday Life in Harappa and Mohenjo-daro

Mohenjo-daro and Harappa were the biggest urban centers in the Indus Valley during the first wave of urbanization. As one might expect, the everyday life of the common people changed in many ways.

For starters, what was once agricultural settlements now became urban centers, with around forty thousand people in each of the cities. Urban planning also became more elaborate, with Mohenjo-daro and Harappa organizing buildings in grids. Public buildings were organized on a citadel mound in the northwest part of the city, and homes were built on the lower, descending part. In Mohenjo-daro, the citadel mound where the public buildings were erected also contained the Great Bath.

The Great Bath in Mohenjo-daro. Credit: Sujay Rao Mandavilli, Institute for the Study of Globalization.

Aside from the discovery of the Great Bath, archaeologists discovered a massive granary where the people of Mohenjo-daro kept their surplus of crops collected during the year. Harappa also had a substantial number of granaries and water tanks as well. Both cities used forts and brick walls to create physical borders that could have served as protection against potential attacks and floods. The houses often had multiple stories, and the lower part of the house could serve as a workshop for artisans and craftsmen. These workshops would seldom be in a separate part of the city that would pose as a working district. All houses and public buildings were built from the same type of brick, which was first dried in the sun then baked before being used for construction projects.

Most of the houses found in the lower part of the city would have private bathrooms and their own baths, which were connected to the public sewage system that took care of the wastewater. People could clean the sewers easily, as the system was built beneath the streets of the city and had covers that could be removed for easy maintenance.

The people of Harappa had experienced metal workers, as there is evidence to support the idea that they made copper and bronze objects, whether they were figurines or cookware. They would also cook and keep their food stored in clay pots, some of which were made with the use of a pottery wheel, while others were made by hand.

The diet of the Harappans and the people of Mohenjo-daro consisted of various grains, like wheat, rice, and barley, and a great variety of fruit and vegetables. They also consumed meat like chicken, cattle, and wild game. Seafood and fish were also a part of their staple foods. A great number of animal bones were found during excavations, which indicates that the people of Harappa and Mohenjo-daro had meat in abundance. They also ate chickpeas, peas, pigeon peas, millet, mustard, sesame seeds, sorghum, chickpea and black pepper chutney, flaxseed with honey, pickled cucumber with cumin, and millet-stuffed spinach leaves.

Cotton was domesticated in this region around 5000 BCE, so the people of Harappa and Mohenjo-daro were most likely skillful at weaving and sewing. Both women and men wore light garments. The upper garment resembled a shawl, and the lower part resembled modern-day dhotis, which were worn by men. Women wore long skirts. Statues like the Priest-King, who is dressed in floral garments, or a goddess with jewels indicate that women might have worn a lot of jewelry and that men liked wearing colorful clothes with ornaments. However, it is not certain whether people dressed like this daily or whether this was only the case for special occasions, such as religious ceremonies and festivals.

The Priest-King, which was found in Mohenjo-daro. Located in the National Museum of Karachi, Pakistan. Credit: Wikimedia Commons.

Goddess in jewels with big earrings. Located in Royal Ontario Museum, Toronto, Ontario, Canada. Credit: Wikimedia Commons.

Clothes weren't only made from cotton; people also used leather, silk, wool, linen, and flax to create garments. Jewelry was made from copper, gold, and different stones and gems.

To pass their free time, people would sing, dance, and swim, as well as play games that resembled chess. Dice games were still popular during this time too. Children would play with a variety of toys, including carts, animal figurines, woolen balls and toys, and board games.

How Alexander the Great Changed Life in India

While Alexander the Great changed the world map and political milieu in the Mediterranean and Indian subcontinent with his war campaigns and conquests, the connection that was established between the two continents also changed the lives of the common people.

As Alexander was preparing for what would become known as one of the greatest war campaigns in history, Macedonian soldiers were tasked with carrying and transporting saffron to Asia and the Indian subcontinent. Saffron would become a staple spice in traditional Asian and Indian dishes. Today, India is the fourth-largest producer of saffron in the world.

Other similarities between Greek and Indian cuisine are tzatziki and Indian sauce, which also involves herbs and garlic. The only difference between the two is that Greeks use yogurt, while curd is used in Indian cuisine. Curd is a product that is made by adding acidic ingredients to milk. Naan bread, a staple food of India, and pita bread, which was made in Greece, are also somewhat similar in style, although they are different types of bread.

The Greeks and the people of the Indian subcontinent shared more connections beyond gastronomy and cuisine. Greeks and Buddhists were both attracted to the idea of a vegetarian diet. Pythagoras taught his students that a vegetarian-based diet had the best effects on the body, while Buddhism preached vegetarianism in the spiritual sense, as it would affect one's reincarnation.

Greeks also introduced Indian cultures to technology and innovations in astronomy and astrology. Chandragupta also incorporated the concept of having a standing army, which wasn't the case before with the Indus Valley civilization.

It is also thought that the concept of coins was introduced to India by Greeks from Bactria. However, the excavation of rectangle coins in mint condition from Taxila, dating around 400 BCE, testifies to a different scenario, where the concept of coinage was already established in the Indian subcontinent, at least in some parts.

One of the biggest legacies of Alexander the Great left behind in India were military colonies that turned into settlements. These were mostly inhabited by the Greek populace. These military bases later became Greek colonies of migrants, who came from the Mediterranean and inhabited the Indian subcontinent.

Sometime around the decline of the Maurya Empire, a period known to history as the Indo-Greek era commenced. For the next two hundred years, Greek kings ruled the Indian subcontinent, and they would combine Hindu and Greek religions, including Buddhism. They would also blend ancient Greek symbols with Indian, as well as art and architecture.

Everyday Life of People in the Maurya Empire

The Maurya Empire was vast and thus had a dual nature of potential high stability and power or a fast decline into havoc. If the empire was ruled by a weak and indecisive king who would place his desires ahead of the empire's needs, the Maurya Empire would decline, as was the case soon after Ashoka's death. If it was ruled by a strong leader, the empire would thrive.

Such an empire would have a complex and elaborate system of governance, as well as a layered caste system, which was the case of the Maurya Empire. The caste system in Maurya wasn't determined based on birth but rather on occupation. Maurya's class system, or caste system, was divided into seven categories. The first of the seven castes were the Brahmins (priests and teachers). There were few Brahmins, but they were very respected, which was noted in

Megasthenes's *Indica*. The second caste consisted of farmers. There were, of course, many farmers in Maurya, and they were well respected. The third caste was shepherds and hunters. Only shepherds and hunters were allowed to trade, breed, and hunt animals. The fourth caste was artisans, day laborers, and traders. The fifth caste was soldiers, and as Megasthenes records in his book, the soldiers would do nothing but drink when they weren't fighting wars for their king. Soldiers were paid from the empire's treasury even if there weren't any wars. The sixth caste consisted of inspectors, who acted as spies and were to report everything they heard to the king himself. The seventh caste was the king's officers who worked at the court or in other public offices. This included ministers, governors, judges, and administrative workers.

The governance system was elaborate, with governors taking care of the surrounding regions and a council of ministers helping the king. There were special tax collectors and census officers who would record the deaths of all the people in the empire, as well as the death of cattle. The purpose of having a census was to follow up with taxes, which filled the empire's treasury.

The Maurya Empire also became one of the main trading centers in the Indian subcontinent and farther, thanks to an ambitious project that the Great Road represented. This highway connected Pataliputra with Taxila, and there are also smaller roads leading to other parts of India. That is how the people of Maurya could easily trade, travel, and establish communication with other cities.

The empire also had officers who kept peace on the streets and took care of criminals, just like present-day police officers. Chandragupta knew that public health was of great importance for the peace and prosperity of his empire, so he made a great number of hospitals and employed doctors, nurses, and midwives. Healthcare was available to everyone, and it was free for all. To avoid food poisoning and cases of malnutrition, the king made food alteration punishable by law.

There were two types of judicial courts: criminal and civil. However, the king made the final decision when it came to judicial matters. The king was considered to be the source of supreme justice. The death sentence could be used, especially in cases of murder and treason. Those who were sentenced to death would offer to give donations before they died so they would have a better life in their next reincarnation.

The position of women in the empire was favorable. Women could become one of the king's guards or work as officials. Women also had the right to their property, which were usually bridal gifts. Moreover, the mistreatment of women was punishable by law. Polygamy was reserved only for monarchs, but common people could marry more than a single woman in case their wife wasn't able to bear any children.

The empire was wealthy, so different types of food, both cultivated and imported, were available except for periods of famine. The empire could even afford a standing army of at least eighty thousand soldiers, who lived off the empire's treasury.

The people of Maurya had a diverse diet, consisting of various dairy products, beverages, meat and wild game, seafood and fish, grain, and fruit and vegetables. More than several types of rice and barley were cultivated within the empire's borders, while the people of Maurya also used masa, which was usually made during the cold season and in-between seasons when different cereals and grain were cultivated in the region. Masa is a form of dough that is used to make all kinds of dishes and delights, including flatbread. The people of Maurya would also make porridge and soups out of different grains and ingredients. Soups were particularly popular and nutritious. Another popular food choice was sugar. The Mauryan people also used honey. Spices were an important part of Mauryan cuisine; they used peppers, cloves, mustard, coriander, turmeric, ginger, cumin, and salt.

The Mauryan people loved their drinks too. They made rice beer and wine, grape juice, fruit syrups, and all kinds of liquor and non-alcoholic beverages.

Compared to the pre-Mauryan period, the people of the Mauryan Empire had more or less a stable lifestyle and could prosper, especially during the reign of Chandragupta and Ashoka the Great.

Chapter 10 – The Cultural Legacy of Ancient India: Art, Architecture, and Religion

While architecture can tell a lot about a civilization, such as its development, technology, and lifestyle, art leaves behind an important cultural heritage. And religion is often a great source of knowledge and information about a civilization lost to the sands of time. What is the cultural legacy of ancient India, and what can art, architecture, and religion reveal about the greatness and beauty of ancient India?

Art and Architecture in Ancient India

As far as the architectural legacy of ancient India is concerned, there aren't many remains that can testify to its greatness. But from the remains of buildings made with sun-dried baked bricks to Megasthenes's description of Chandragupta's magnificent palace with elaborate wood carvings and ornaments, it is difficult not to believe that even more magnificent buildings are now lost and forgotten to the tooth of relentless time and decay.

Dholavira ruins, western India, Gujarat. Credit: Wikimedia Commons.

Megasthenes's *Indica* was not the only ancient book that talked about arts and architecture in India. The *Manasara* is one of the most cherished texts on architecture, and it reveals details on the principles used in the sculpture and architecture of ancient India.

Not all construction projects were meant to be pretty; sometimes, they were meant to be useful and strong. After all, ancient Indian masons built tall walls and forts for protection. Many cities from the time of the Harappa civilization started to erect tall forts and walls around their borders to prevent floods and intrusions and to create a defense against potential attacks.

Rajgir city walls dating from around the 6ᵗʰ century BCE, Magadh region, Bihar. Credit: Wikimedia Commons.

A great number of seals with ornaments and different symbols, such as animals, also testify to an early inclination toward art and artistic forms. Thousands of stamp seals were retrieved during numerous excavations since the discovery of cities like Mohenjo-daro and Harappa.

The Pashupati seal, Indus Valley civilization, Mohenjo-daro, around 2500 BCE. The seal depicts a seated creature surrounded by animals. Credit: Wikimedia Commons.

One of the most famous seals is the Pashupati seal, which was excavated in the Mohenjo-daro archaeological site and dates from around 2500 BCE. The seal shows a seated or throned human-like creature surrounded by all kinds of animals, including a bison, tiger, and goats. The scene might depict a deity from the early days of the Indus Valley civilization.

A great number of seals were found later in Harappa and across the Indian subcontinent in the former centers of some of the first civilizations. Most of them depict animals. The seals might have had a ceremonial and religious reason, while some might have been used as trading tags for merchandising purposes.

The golden age of art in ancient India would probably be the Mauryan era, especially during the period of Ashoka's reign. While Ashoka's grandfather and the founder of the Maurya Empire, Chandragupta, mostly commissioned wooden buildings and objects that didn't survive the test of time but were remembered in some scriptures, Ashoka created stone buildings and sculptures across the empire. Many of Ashoka's pillar and stone edicts remain intact. They were excavated hundreds of years after Ashoka's death.

Ashoka built stupas, which are religious monuments. There, Buddha's relics and remains were kept by the will of Ashoka. Ancient writers attribute Ashoka as the founder of over eighty-four thousand stupas across the Indian subcontinent.

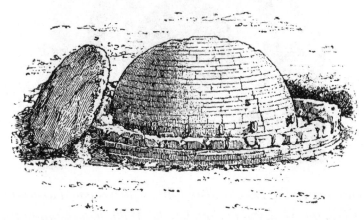

A form of an early stupa, probably built during the Maurya Empire around the 3ᵈ century BCE outside Chakdara, Pakistan. Credit: Wikimedia Commons.

Ashoka also commissioned the building and decorating of pillars, rock-cut caves, and palaces. One of the most famous and legendary palaces that are said to have been built during Ashoka's time is Ashoka's Hell—a prison building that looked like the most beautiful palace in the world but hid unimaginable horrors of blood, gore, and torture. The remains of this supposed palace were never found, which is why its existence is speculated.

The most famous group of caves cut from a massive rock formation and attributed to Ashoka has to be the Barabar Hill Caves, located in Bihar, India, specifically in the region of Makhdumpur. The caves might have been commissioned by Ashoka but were finished later during the reign of his grandson, Dasharatha. The Lomas Rishi Cave dates from around 250 BCE and is the oldest surviving rock-cut architecture.

The entrance to the Lomas Rishi Cave, which is dated to around 250 BCE, the Mauryan period. Credit: Wikimedia Commons.

The caves were often decorated with sculptures of ancient ascetics and depicted important lessons of Dharma and Buddhism, including Nirvana, also known as Parinirvana. Therefore, art and architecture were often used as mediums for religious education and spiritual enlightenment.

A sculpture of an ascetic of the Ajivika cult, commissioned by the Mauryan dynasty between the 3ʳᵈ and 2ⁿᵈ century BCE. Credit: Wikimedia Commons.

The entrance corridor of Sudama cave, one of the caves carved into Barabar Hill. Credit: Wikimedia Commons.

The city of Pataliputra was the capital of the Maurya Empire, and it was decorated with lavish architecture whose remains were discovered during the excavations. Pataliputra was a major city that had between 150,000 and 400,000 inhabitants during the reign of Ashoka. Some of the most significant architectural remains from the Mauryan era were found in the archaeological site of Kumrahar, where the ancient city of Pataliputra was once located. As Megasthenes writes about the Mauryan capital, the city had nearly six hundred towers and sixty-four gates.

Ruins of a hall with the pillars intact at the Kumrahar site (Pataliputra). It was built during the Mauryan era around the 3rd century BCE. Credit: Wikimedia Commons.

The splendor and magnificence of the Mauryan capital can be imagined based on some of the architectural remains, among which is the Pataliputra palace chapiter.

The Pataliputra chapiter, which was excavated in the ruins of the Mauryan palace in Pataliputra. It has been dated to between the 4th and 3[d] century BCE. Credit: Wikimedia Commons.

The chapiter, another name for the capital, was the part of the pillar that supported the structure. The chapiter has some elements of Greek architecture, which confirms the influence of Hellenistic styles and art on the culture in ancient India. The main motif on the Pataliputra chapiter is a flame palmette, with supporting decorative elements such as bead and reel patterns and rosettes on the top edge.

Many architectural and artistic finds, especially pieces dating from the Mauryan era, are closely related to religion.

Religion in Ancient India

During the pre-Vedic and Vedic periods, the people of ancient India believed in the spiritualism of female and male principles, as well as natural forces. The creative human nature, with its ability to make, create, and imagine, was also considered sacred. The people of the Indus Valley civilization would often attribute characteristics of the divine to natural forces, such as the sun and the moon. Some of the scriptures in Vedic culture, like the *Rig Veda*, reveal that Indo-Aryans had numerous deities and followed a polytheistic religion. The main way of worshiping these sacred entities was through rituals of offerings. For instance, they would offer food to fire to honor gods like Agni, Varuna, Rudra, Indra, and Surya, which are all deities of Hinduism.

A depiction of Agni, the god of fire, riding a goat. Credit: Wikimedia Commons.

Agni is the Hindu deity that represents fire and serves as the protector of men. Indra is the god of war, thunder, storms, rain, lightning, and rivers. Varuna is believed to be the lord of the sky and seas, and he later became a god of justice and truth. Rudra is the deity of wind, storms, and hunting, and Surya is the god of the sun and the father of other deities, such as the god of death, Yama.

*A 1940s artwork that depicts Surya, the god of the sun, light, and day.
Credit: Wikimedia Commons.*

What makes the thought and philosophy of ancient India different
from Western thought is a deeper insight into the nature of the soul,
spiritualism, and the overall meaning of life and all its intricacies. Due
to India's numerous reforms of spiritualism, religion, and philosophy,
it transformed into a colorful cloth of different faiths.

One of the oldest religions in India is Jainism. Jainism relies on the
three sacred pillars of nonviolence, non-attachment, and non-
absolutism. Jains were predominantly vegetarian, as they followed a
vow of nonviolence, and there are other practices within the religion,

like sexual constraints, a vow not to steal, restraining from owning too many possessions, and dedicating one's life to serve the truth.

The official symbol of Jainism. Credit: Wikimedia Commons.

Jainism is neither theistic nor atheistic. Instead, it can be considered a spiritual philosophy that goes beyond these two concepts, thus categorizing it as transtheistic. Moreover, Jainism is one of the oldest continuous religions that have survived the test of time; it is still being practiced in some parts of India. According to Jainism, the world exists perpetually and was not created by a god or a sacred entity but is independent and will exist forever. Like Buddhism, which came later to the religious scene of Asia with the teachings of Siddhartha Gautama, Jains believe in reincarnation, i.e., being born again as a mortal.

The swastika is a significant symbol of Jainism, and it was later adopted by other ethnicities and religions, like Buddhism.

Seals with swastika symbols that were found in the Indus Valley; they are today located in the British Museum. Credit: Wikimedia Commons.

The dual nature of a swastika represents the dual nature of Brahma, the god who created the universe and everything within it. A swastika that is facing right signifies the evolution of the universe; if the swastika faces left, it represents the involution of it. In Hinduism, the swastika signifies the deity Vishnu and the sun rays that give life to every breathing creature on the earth.

Hinduism is the third largest religion in the world, with most of its followers living in India.

Buddhism originated in the 5th century BCE, and as mentioned before, it also adopted the swastika as a symbol. There is a story of Buddha's disciples stamping a swastika on his chest after he died. The stamp is known as the Heart's Seal. One of the most compelling religious teachings was preached by Siddhartha Gautama, who later became known as Buddha. A young prince found the truth about worldly pleasures and sufferings, so he quit his life of comfort and luxury to lead an ascetic life and dedicated his existence to teaching people about the noble ways of Dharma. Buddhism was one of the largest religions in ancient India since its founding. One of the greatest kings in the history of India, Ashoka, was a great devotee.

The edicts of Ashoka and over eighty-four thousand stupas were commissioned and built to spread the word of Buddhism. Ashoka's change of heart was also a popular story among Buddhists of the time, as they wanted to emphasize how Buddhism could change people for the better. Today, around eight million people in India are Buddhists, which is less than 1 percent of the present-day population in India. However, Buddhism is the fourth largest religion in the world, with China boasting the largest Buddhist population.

Even though Ashoka was a proclaimed Buddhist, there were many different religions practiced within the borders of the great Mauryan Empire, including Jainism. There was another religious cult in ancient India called Zoroastrianism, but it is not known whether this sect converged from Buddhism or Jainism. Zoroastrianism is an old religion, possibly drawing origins from the 2nd millennium BCE. The first written evidence of this religion and its Iranian prophet, Zoroaster, appear in the 5th century BCE. Zoroastrianism is a combination of theology and philosophy, proscribing good words, good deeds, and good thoughts so that people can fight evil with the goodness in their hearts. This religion is still around today, making it one of the world's oldest continuously practicing religions.

At last, with frequent and large-scale migrations of ancient Greeks to the Indian subcontinent, the Maurya Empire saw a rise of religious followers of Greek polytheism. This created a clash of different myths, legends, thoughts, philosophies, and spiritual beliefs, making ancient India a unique cultural ecosystem with a rich historical legacy.

Conclusion

From the first sign of a thriving civilization that bloomed thanks to elaborate irrigation systems and developing agriculture on the banks of the Indus River to the founding of one of the largest empires in world history, ancient India went through radical changes within seven thousand years.

Due to India's complex evolution, we can now enjoy myths, legends, and attested historical facts fueled by what is left of once-great empires and pioneer settlements of civilization.

Even though we only have a glimpse into the world and life of ancient India, it is not difficult to imagine the splendor and richness of the Maurya Empire or the fearlessness and ambition of Alexander the Great, who came to this beautiful land with dreams of conquering the world.

We are glad you went on this trip to the past to learn more about the marvelous Indian subcontinent. Hopefully, this book has piqued your interest to learn even more about India's evolution. After all, the history of civilization cannot be lost if it is not forgotten.

Here's another book by Captivating History that you might like

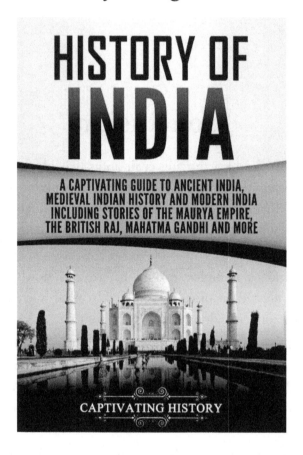

Free Bonus from Captivating History
(Available for a Limited time)

Hi History Lovers!

Now you have a chance to join our exclusive history list so you can get your first history ebook for free as well as discounts and a potential to get more history books for free! Simply visit the link below to join.

Captivatinghistory.com/ebook

Also, make sure to follow us on Facebook, Twitter and Youtube by searching for Captivating History.

References

Allchin, B. and Allchin, R. 1982. *The Birth of Indian Civilization.* Cambridge: Cambridge University Press.

Thapar, Romila. 2002. *Early India: From the Origins to CE 1300.* Penguin.

Pletcher, Kenneth. 2010. *The History of India.* The Rosen Publishing Group.

Gauranga Nath, Benerjee. 1966. *Hellenism in India.* Farber and Farber LTD, London.

E.J. Rapson. 1922. *Cambridge History of India, Ancient India Vol. 2.* Cambridge.

Allchin, F. Raymond, ed. 1995. *The Archaeology of Early Historic South Asia: The Emergence of Cities and States.* New York: Cambridge University Press.

Guruge, Ananda W. P. 1993. *Ashoka, the Righteous: A Definitive Biography.* Central Cultural Fund.

Romesh Chunder Dutt. 2013. *A History of Civilization in Ancient India, Based on Sanskrit Literature, Vol. 2.* Routledge.

Ram Sharan Sharma. 2005. *India's Ancient Past.* Oxford University Press.

Klaus Klostermaier. 1999. *Buddhism: A Short Introduction.*

Robin Lane Fox. 1980. *The Search for Alexander.* Little Brown & Co. Boston.

Arrian. 1971. *The Campaigns of Alexander.* Translated by Aubrey de Selincourt, London, Penguin books.

Gokhale, Balkirshna Govind. 1966. *Ashoka Maurya.* New York, Twayne Publishers.

K.A. Nilakanta Sastri. 1996. *Age of the Nandas and Mauryas.* Motilal Banarsidass.

Radha Kumud Mookerji. 2016. *Chandragupta Maurya and His Times.* Motilal Banarsidass.

Made in the USA
Las Vegas, NV
06 August 2022

52808167R10075